First World War
and Army of Occupation
War Diary
France, Belgium and Germany

56 DIVISION
169 Infantry Brigade
London Regiment
9th (County of London) Battalion (Queen Victoria's Rifles)
1 February 1916 - 30 January 1918

WO95/2963/1

The Naval & Military Press Ltd
www.nmarchive.com
Published in association with The National Archives

Published by

The Naval & Military Press Ltd

Unit 10 Ridgewood Industrial Park,

Uckfield, East Sussex,

TN22 5QE England

Tel: +44 (0) 1825 749494

www.naval-military-press.com

www.nmarchive.com

This diary has been reprinted in facsimile from the original. Any imperfections are inevitably reproduced and the quality may fall short of modern type and cartographic standards.

© **Crown Copyright**
Images reproduced by permission of The National Archives, London, England, 2015.

Contents

Document type	Place/Title	Date From	Date To
Heading	WO95/2963/1 1/9 Battalion London Regiment (Queen Victorial Rifles)		
Heading	56th Division 169th Infy Bde 1-9th Bn London Regt Feb 1916-Jan 1918		
War Diary	Talmas	01/02/1916	08/02/1916
War Diary	Cardonnette	09/02/1916	13/02/1916
War Diary	Fresne	14/02/1916	27/02/1916
War Diary	Ailly	28/02/1916	11/03/1916
War Diary	Fienvillers	12/03/1916	14/03/1916
War Diary	Doullens	15/03/1916	15/03/1916
War Diary	Houvin-Houvigneul	16/03/1916	01/05/1916
War Diary	Dainville	02/05/1916	04/05/1916
War Diary	Houvin	05/05/1916	06/05/1916
War Diary	Halloy	07/05/1916	19/05/1916
War Diary	St Amand	20/05/1916	20/05/1916
War Diary	Sailly	21/05/1916	27/05/1916
War Diary	Hebuterne	28/05/1916	08/06/1916
War Diary	Halloy	09/06/1916	13/06/1916
War Diary	Sailly Hebuterne	14/06/1916	21/06/1916
War Diary	Halloy	22/06/1916	27/06/1916
War Diary	St Amand	28/06/1916	30/06/1916
Operation(al) Order(s)	Q.V.R. Attack Order No. 1	27/06/1916	27/06/1916
Miscellaneous	Appendix Showing Tools Etc Carried		
Heading	169th Brigade 56th Division 1/9th Battalion London Regiment July 1916		
War Diary	(St Amand) Hebuterne	01/07/1916	01/07/1916
War Diary	Bayencourt	02/07/1916	02/07/1916
War Diary	St Amand	03/07/1916	05/07/1916
War Diary	Fonquevillers	06/07/1916	14/07/1916
War Diary	Hannescamp	15/07/1916	19/07/1916
War Diary	Bienvillers & Fonquevillers	20/07/1916	30/07/1916
War Diary	St. Amand	31/07/1916	31/07/1916
Miscellaneous	Report On Operations At Gommecourt	01/07/1916	01/07/1916
Heading	169th Brigade 56th Division 1/9th Battalion London Regiment (Q.V.R) August 1916		
War Diary	St. Amand	01/08/1916	06/08/1916
War Diary	Fonquevillers	07/08/1916	15/08/1916
War Diary	Fonquevillers & Bienvillers	15/08/1916	18/08/1916
War Diary	Beaudricourt	19/08/1916	21/08/1916
War Diary	Villers L'Hopital	22/08/1916	22/08/1916
War Diary	Argenvillers	23/08/1916	31/08/1916
Heading	169th Brigade 56th Division 1/9th Battalion London Regiment September 1916.		
War Diary	Argenvillers	01/09/1916	02/09/1916
War Diary	Corbie	03/09/1916	30/09/1916
Heading	1/9 London Regt. Vol XVII		
War Diary	Carnoy & Lesboeufs	01/10/1916	03/10/1916
War Diary	Fricourt	04/10/1916	11/10/1916
War Diary	Picquigny	12/10/1916	20/10/1916
War Diary	Limeux	21/10/1916	23/10/1916

War Diary	St Venant	23/10/1916	23/10/1916
War Diary	Lestrem	24/10/1916	26/10/1916
War Diary	Bout Deville	27/10/1916	31/10/1916
Miscellaneous	Narrative Of Operations	14/10/1916	14/10/1916
War Diary	Neuve Chapelle	01/11/1916	02/11/1916
War Diary	Bout Deville	03/11/1916	08/11/1916
War Diary	Neuve Chapelle	09/11/1916	14/11/1916
War Diary	Croix Barbee	15/11/1916	20/11/1916
War Diary	Neuve Chapelle	21/11/1916	26/11/1916
War Diary	La Gorgue	27/11/1916	08/12/1916
War Diary	Neuve Chapelle	09/12/1916	14/12/1916
War Diary	Pont Du Hem & Rouge Croix	16/12/1916	20/12/1916
War Diary	Neuve Chapelle	21/12/1916	26/12/1916
War Diary	Pont Du Hem	27/12/1916	01/01/1917
War Diary	Robermetz	02/01/1917	13/01/1917
War Diary	Laventie	14/01/1917	28/02/1917
War Diary	La Gorgue	01/03/1917	01/03/1917
War Diary	St. Floris	02/03/1917	07/03/1917
War Diary	Gouy-En-Artois	08/03/1917	13/03/1917
War Diary	Arras	14/03/1917	17/03/1917
War Diary	Achicourt	18/03/1917	31/03/1917
Miscellaneous	War Diary For 9th London Regt	03/05/1917	03/05/1917
War Diary	Monchiet	01/04/1917	30/04/1917
Miscellaneous	Administrative Instructions	05/04/1917	05/04/1917
Miscellaneous	Q.V.R. Instructions No.4	06/04/1917	06/04/1917
Miscellaneous	Q.V.R. Instructions No.6	07/04/1917	07/04/1917
War Diary		01/05/1917	20/05/1917
War Diary	Duisans	20/05/1917	23/05/1917
War Diary	Agnez-Les Duisans	24/05/1917	20/06/1917
War Diary	Beaurains	21/06/1917	01/07/1917
War Diary	Gouy	02/07/1917	02/07/1917
War Diary	Sus-St. Leger	03/07/1917	24/07/1917
War Diary	Nortleulinghem	25/07/1917	31/07/1917
Heading	War Diary Of 1/9th Battn The London Regt (Queen Victoria's Rifles)		
War Diary	Nortleulinghem	01/08/1917	05/08/1917
War Diary	Watou	06/08/1917	31/08/1917
Miscellaneous	Headquarters 56th Division.	20/08/1917	20/08/1917
Miscellaneous	Replies To G3/846		
Miscellaneous	No.5 Platoon		
Miscellaneous	Attack Report		
Miscellaneous	No.7 Platoon		
Miscellaneous	8. Platoon B. Coy Q.V.R.		
Miscellaneous	Report By "Mopping Up"		
Heading	1/9 London Regt Vol XXI		
Heading	War Diary Of 1/9th Bn The London Regt From 1st September 1917 To 30th September 1917 Vol 34		
War Diary	Bapaume	01/09/1917	04/09/1917
War Diary	Lebucquiere	05/09/1917	30/09/1917
Heading	War Diary Of 1/9th Bn The London Regt From 1st October 1917 To 31st October 1917 Vol 35		
War Diary		01/10/1917	31/10/1917
Heading	War Diary 1/9th London Regt. November 1917 Vol 36		
Miscellaneous	Cover For Documents. Nature Of Enclosures.		
War Diary	Lebucquiere	01/11/1917	30/11/1917

Heading	War Diary 1/9th London Regt (Q.V.R.) December 1917 Vol 37		
War Diary		01/12/1917	31/12/1917
Heading	War Diary Of 1/9th Bn London Regt Queen Victoria's Rifles From 1st January 1918 To 30th January 1918 Volume I		
War Diary		01/01/1918	30/01/1918

WO/95/2963/1

1/9 Battalion London Regiment
(Queen Victoria's Rifles)

56TH DIVISION
169TH INFY BDE

1-9TH BN LONDON REGT

FEB 1916-JAN 1918

FROM 5 DIV
13 BDE.

To 58 DIV 175 BDE
Absorbed 2/7 Bn

Army Form C. 2118.

WAR DIARY
or
INTELLIGENCE SUMMARY.

Queen Victorias Rifles 1/9th Battn. Lond. Regt.

(Erase heading not required.)

Instructions regarding War Diaries and Intelligence Summaries are contained in F. S. Regs., Part II. and the Staff Manual respectively. Title pages will be prepared in manuscript.

Place	Date	Hour	Summary of Events and Information	Remarks and references to Appendices
TALMAS	1916 FEB. 1		Battalion in billets at TALMAS. 14th Warwicks in adjoining billets.	MAP. 1/00000 LENS. Sheet 11 D.6.
	2		Company drill, open order. Village & wood fighting. Musketry. Class 9. Instruction for junior N.C.Os. Grenade practice.	
	3			
	4			
	5			
	6			
	7			
	8		Battalion marched from TALMAS (leaving 10.30 a.m.) to billets at CARDONNETTE (arriving 12.55 p.m.)	
CARDONNETTE	9		Battalion attack practice. Company training - open order drill. Musketry.	MAP. 1/00000 AMIENS Sheet 14 E.1.
	10			
	11			
	12		Battalion marched from CARDONNETTE (leaving 10.30 a.m.) to billets at PICQUIGNY (arriving 4.30 p.m.) Distance 14 miles. Battalion left 13th Inf. Brigade, 5th Division.	
	13		Battalion marched from PICQUIGNY (leaving 10.0 a.m.) via AIRAINES to billets at VAUX-MARQUENNEVILLE & FRESNE (arriving 4.30 p.m.) Distance 20 miles. Hd. Qrs. at FRESNE. Battalion joined 169th Inf. Brigade 56th Divn.	

J. C. Williams Capt. & Adjt.
for O.C. Queen Victoria Rifles. 1/9th Battn. Lond. Regt.

Army Form C. 2118.

WAR DIARY
or
INTELLIGENCE SUMMARY.
(Erase heading not required.)

Instructions regarding War Diaries and Intelligence Summaries are contained in F. S. Regs., Part II. and the Staff Manual respectively. Title pages will be prepared in manuscript.

Place	Date	Hour	Summary of Events and Information	Remarks and references to Appendices
	1916			
FRESNE	FEB 14		Battalion billets, Hd.Qrs. + 2 Companies at VAUX - MARQUENNEVILLE.	MAP 80000 ABBEVILLE 45° E. 62° N.
	15			
	16			{ Draft arrived { 99 Other Ranks
	17			
	18		Company training. Village fighting. Musketry. Grenade Practice. Trench digging.	
	19			
	20			
	21			
	22			
	23			
	24			
	25			
	26			
	27		Battalion marched from FRESNE (leaving 6.30 a.m.) to AILLY-LE HAUT-CLOCHER (arriving 3.30 pm) 2nd London Regiment and Queen Westminster Rifles in adjoining billets.	MAP 80000 AMIENS 12. FRANCE 1.
AILLY	28			
	29			

K.W.Adams Capt. as Adjt.
for O.C. Queen Victorias Rifles, 1/9th Battn London Regt.

Army Form C. 2118.

169/5/6

WAR DIARY
1/9th Battn. Lond Regt. Queen Victorias Rifles
or INTELLIGENCE SUMMARY.

(Erase heading not required.)

Instructions regarding War Diaries and Intelligence Summaries are contained in F. S. Regs. Part II, and the Staff Manual respectively. Title pages will be prepared in manuscript.

Place	Date	Hour	Summary of Events and Information	Remarks and references to Appendices
AILLY	1916 MAR. 1		Battalion in billets	MAP 80000 AMIENS 12 Point 109.
	2			
	3			
	4			
	5			
	6		Company training. Battalion attack practice, including exhibition attack before Brigadier-General, 169th Infantry Brigade. Grenadiers practice and tests. Training of snipers. Musketry.	
	7			
	8			
	9			
	10			
	11			
FIENVILLERS	12		Battalion marched from AILLY (leaving 4·45 am) to FIENVILLERS (arriving 12·30 pm)	MAP 70000 LENS 11 (C) (3) (D) (3)
	13			
	14			
DOULLENS	15		Battalion marched from FIENVILLERS (leaving 9·30 am) to DOULLENS (arriving 12·0 noon)	DOULLENS 11 (E) (6) (E) (3)
HOUVIN-HOUVIGNEUL	16		Battalion marched from DOULLENS (leaving 8·40 am) to HOUVIN-HOUVIGNEUL (arriving 12·30 pm)	

M.D. Dickins Lieut-Col
O.C. Queen Victorias Rifles.

WAR DIARY
or
INTELLIGENCE SUMMARY.
(Erase heading not required.)

Army Form C. 2118.

Place	Date	Hour	Summary of Events and Information	Remarks and references to Appendices
HOUVIN-HOUVIGNEUL	1916 MAR. 17		Battalion in billets.	MAP 700000 LENS 1 (E) 3
	18		Draft of 5 Officers arrived	
	19			
	20			
	21		Company training. Grenade practice and tests. Battalion attack practice	
	22		Training of snipers. Digging of practice trenches. Musketry	
	23		Draft of 38 Other Ranks arrived.	
	24			
	25			
	26			
	27			
	28			
	29			
	30			
	31			

Lieut-Col.
O.C. Queen Victoria's Rifles

Army Form C. 2118.

WAR DIARY
1/9th Battn. Lond. Regt. Queen Victoria Rifles
INTELLIGENCE SUMMARY.

(Erase heading not required.)

Instructions regarding War Diaries and Intelligence Summaries are contained in F. S. Regs. Part II. and the Staff Manual respectively. Title pages will be prepared in manuscript.

Place	Date	Hour	Summary of Events and Information	Remarks and references to Appendices
HOUVIN-HOUVIGNEUL	1916 APRIL 1		Battalion in billets.	MAP 1/00000 LEN 11 (E) (3)
	2			
	3			
	4			
	5			
	6			
	7		Company and Battalion training. Route marches and musketry. Grenade practice and tests. Bayonet training. Training of snipers.	
	8			
	9			
	10			
	11			
	12			
	13			
	14			
	15			
	16			

R. Woodward Cox. Capt.
O.C. Queen Victoria Rifles.

WAR DIARY
or
INTELLIGENCE SUMMARY.

(Erase heading not required.)

Army Form C. 2118.

Place	Date	Hour	Summary of Events and Information	Remarks and references to Appendices
HOUVIN-HOUVIGNEUL	1916 APRIL 17		Battalion in billets.	
	18			
	19			
	20			
	21			
	22			
	23		Company and Battalion training.	
	24			
	25			
	26			
	27			
	28			
	29			
	30			

R. Woodroffe Cox. Capt.
O.C. Queen Victoria Rifles.

Army Form C. 2118.

WAR DIARY 1/9th Battn. Lond. Regt. Queen Victorias Rifles.
or
INTELLIGENCE SUMMARY.

(Erase heading not required.)

1/9 London R Vol 18

Place	Date	Hour	Summary of Events and Information	Remarks and references to Appendices
HOUVIN	1916 MAY 1		Battalion marched from HOUVIN (leaving 9.30am) to billets in DAINVILLE (arriving 7.30 pm)	MAP 1/100000 LENS 11 (E) (5) (1) (3)
HOUVIGNEUL	2			
DAINVILLE	3		Digging and R.E. fatigues.	
	4		Battalion marched from DAINVILLE (leaving 8.30pm) to original billets in HOUVIN (arriving 6.0am 5.5.16)	
HOUVIN	5			
	6			
	7		Battn. marched with Bde. from HOUVIN (leaving 10.0am) to huts near at HALLOY-in-y-t-corps area (arriving 5.30pm.)	(F) (5)
HALLOY	8			
	9			
	10			
	11		Company training - route marches, bayonet and physical drill. Practice operations at night, trench digging, training of bombers and snipers.	
	12			
	13			
	14			
	15			
	16			

M.P. Dickins Lieut. Col.
O.C. Queen Victorias Rifles.

WAR DIARY
or
INTELLIGENCE SUMMARY.
(Erase heading not required.)

Army Form C. 2118.

Place	Date	Hour	Summary of Events and Information	Casualties Offs.	Casualties O. RKS.	Remarks and references to Appendices
	1916 MAY					
HALLOY	17		Company training. Training of Bombers and Snipers.			
	18					
	19					
ST AMAND	20		Battn. marched from HALLOY (leaving 4.10pm) & billets in ST AMAND (arriving 10.0pm)			MAP 1/100,000 LENS 11
SAILLY	21		Battn. marched from ST AMAND (leaving 1.0pm) H.Qrs & 2 Companies to billets at SAILLY-AU-BOIS, 2 Companies to KEEP, HEBUTERNE, relieving 1st Battn. London Regt.			Ⓐ ⑤ Ⓑ " ⑤
	22		22nd - 24th Battalion in Reserve. Digging and R.E. fatigues			
	23		Draft 4/3 other Ranks arrived			
	24					
	25					
	26		Draft 6 other Ranks arrived. Billets shelled.		3 Killed 22 Wnded	
	27					
HEBUTERNE	28		Battn. relieved 1/5th Lond. Regt (L.R.B.) H.H. Qrs & 2 Coyrs in Rugmels. 2 Coyrs in trenches Y 47 - 50.		2 Killed 14 Wnded	Ⓑ ⑤
	29		4th Battn. London Fusiliers on right, Poth. & Rugby Regt (48th Divn) on left flank.	-	1 Killed 1 Killed 5 Killed 14 Wnded	
	30			-	3 Killed 5 Wnded	
	31		Draft 5 Officers arrived			

M.P. Dickins
Lieut. Col.
O.C. Queen Victoria's Rifles.

Army Form C. 2118.

9th Battn. Lond. Regt. Queen Victoria Rifles

WAR DIARY
INTELLIGENCE SUMMARY.
(Erase heading not required.)

Vol 19

Place	Date	Hour	Summary of Events and Information	Casualties Officers	Casualties O. Ranks	Remarks and references to Appendices
HEBUTERNE	1916 JUNE 1		Hd Qrs. + 2 Coys. in Dugouts. 2 Coys. in Trenches Y.4.Y-50.		1 Killed 16 Wounded	MAP 1/10,000 LENS 11 (H) (S)
	2			1		
	3		2 Coys. in trenches relieved by 2 nd trenches	1	2 Wounded 1 Killed 2 Wounded	
	4			1 Wounded		
	5					
	6		Battalion in reserve, HEBUTERNE Keep. RE. + digging fatigues			
	7					
	8		Battn. relieved by 14th Lond. Regt. (London Scottish) & marched to HALLOY.			
HALLOY	9					-- (F) (S)
	10		Battalion attack practice.			
	11					
	12					
	13		Battalion marched from HALLOY (leaving 4.0 p.m.) - Hd. Qrs. + 2 Coys. to SAILLY-AU-BOIS, 2 Coys. to HEBUTERNE			
SAILLY & HEBUTERNE	14					
	15					

[signature] Lieut Col.
O.C. Queen Victoria's Rifles

WAR DIARY or INTELLIGENCE SUMMARY.

(Erase heading not required.)

Army Form C. 2118.

Place	Date	Hour	Summary of Events and Information	Casualties Officers	Casualties O. Ranks	Remarks and references to Appendices
SAILLY-HEBUTERNE	1916 JUNE 16		Battalion engaged in digging BOYAU-DE-SERVICE and other assembly trenches. C.T.s. R.E. fatigues.			
	17				1 Wounded	
	18					
	19				2 Wounded	
	20				1 Wounded	
	21		Battalion marched from SAILLY + HEBUTERNE to huts/tents at HALLOY			
HALLOY	22		Attack Practice. Trench digging. R.E. Fatigues			
	23					
	24					
	25					
	26					
	27		Battalion marched from HALLOY to billets at ST. AMAND		1 Wounded	MAP 1/10000 LENS II Ⓐ Ⓑ
ST AMAND	28		Battalion in Reserve.			
	29					
	30					

[signature] Lieut. Col.
O.C. Queen Victoria Rifles.

SECRET

Ref: 1/10000
HEBUTERNE
FONQUEVILLERS

Q.V.R ATTACK ORDER Nº 7. Copy Nº

1. The VII Corps intention is to establish itself on a line which runs approximately from our present front line — 250ˣ N.E. of 16 POPLARS — E. of NAMELESS FM — along ridge in K.5a & E.29c — Little Z. & thence back to own line. 46ᵗʰ Div. attacks from the N.W. & 56ᵗʰ Div. from S.W. The two Divisions to meet about E.29.c.6.0.
The 168ᵗʰ Bde will attack on the right of the 169ᵗʰ. The left of the 168 Bde will rest on a point FELL 50ˣ N.W. of trench junction K.5.c.5.2. They will establish a strong point about cross trenches of FELL and FELON with EPTE.

2. The task of the 169ᵗʰ Bde will be carried out in 4 phases.
   1ˢᵗ Phase. To capture from left of 168ᵗʰ Bde., along FELL, FELLOW, FEUD, CEMETERY, ECK, MAZE, EEL and FIR and establish 3 strong points viz:— (1) near CEMETERY
   (2) at the MAZE
   (3) at S.E. corner of GOMMECOURT PARK.
   2ⁿᵈ Phase. (immediately after 1ˢᵗ) to clean EMS, ETCH and capture the quadrilateral.
   3ʳᵈ Phase. (immediately after 2ⁿᵈ) to secure cross trenches at K.5.a.7.8. clean INDUS cross FILL & FILLET to join hands with 16ᵗʰ Div. along FILL & consolidate FILLET facing E.
   4ᵗʰ Phase. (to commence 3 hrs after Zero) To clear both GOMMECOURT VILLAGE and PARK in a N.W. direction from line FIR – EEL – MAZE – ECK – CEMETERY.
   46ᵗʰ Div. will clear the Village in a S.E. direction. Further details later.

3. **Assembly of Battalion.**
   A } in Y.47 & Boyau
   C
   1 platoon 5ᵗʰ Cheshires & 8 R.E. (attached C Coy) Boyau
   B   in Y.47 L. left & right of YANKEE ST.
   D   in Y.47 R. in Reserve.

4. **Advance Formation.**
   1ˢᵗ wave   A   1 platoon } from right to left at 4 paces interval
               C   1   "
   2ⁿᵈ wave   A   2   "   }   "   "   "   2   "   "
               C   2   "
   3ʳᵈ wave   A   1   "   }   "   "   "   4   "   "
               C   1   "
   4ᵗʰ wave.   3 sections B bombers }
               1 platoon Cheshires. }   "   "   "   2   "   "
               8 sappers R.E.   }

Pioneers & Sappers will remain in FEED until required.

5th Wave. B. 4 platoons } in line at 2 paces interval.
T.M.B. ½ Sect. }
Signallers }

6th Wave. D.

5. **Objectives.**

A. through FEVER, FEINT to FELL and FELLOW.
C. " FERN. EMS (incl.) FEED and EMDEN to FEUD. STRONG POINT, CEMETERY. As soon as STRONG POINT is established and EMS is clear, 1 platoon C in FEUD will occupy EMS, getting in touch with QWR at QUADRILATERAL.

Platoons of A in FELLOW & FELL will move to their left & be in support in FEUD & FELLOW.

B. " FEVER FERN to FEINT FEED.

6. **Company Bombers.**

A clear FEINT, FELL, FELLOW, ETCH above FELL until in touch with QWR
C clear FEED, FEUD, EMDEN & EMS above FEUD.
B " FEVER FERN.

7. **H.Q. Bombers.**

1 group clear each each of the C.T's ETCH, EMS, EMDEN from front line to 3rd line.

8. **Lewis Guns**

2 L.G will be attached to each Coy & under the command of O.C. Coys.
Lewis guns will not fire unless necessary, until the trenches are consolidated & position occupied, except in case of counter-attack.

9. **Contact Patrols**

A & C will find contact patrols to keep in touch with 168 Bde on our right (Left Batt = Rangers) and L.R.B on our left respectively

10. **Stretcher Bearers.**

8 with 5th wave, 8 at Dressing Station.

11. **Communications.**

(a) Telephonic
(b) Visual
(c) Runners.
(d) C's

(a) Telephonic — a Report Centre (R.C) is established at the junction of YELLOW st & front line, connected to Batt. HQ. by D5 cable (2 lines)

Assault.
(1) 4 Signallers will carry across wires in duplicate to establish an Advanced Report Centre (A.R.C) at the junction of EMS and FEED. Similarly L.Q.B. establish A.R.C up EXE
Q.W.R. " " " ETCH.

The calls for these are ETCH on the right = R
EMS   centre   = C
EXE   left   = L.

(2) 4 Signallers will establish 'phone station in FEINT 50' N.W of junction of FEINT and EPTE.

(3) 4 Signallers will lay line up ETCH, and laterally one along FEED to A.R.C
" " FEINT to FEINT phone station.

(4) 8 Signallers at R.C for line work. Part of this personnel will also lay rabbit netting across No Mans Land.
Batt. Signallers will man R.C from 11 a.m. Y day.

At all trench junctions in German 2nd line notice boards will be fixed denoting direction of A.R.C & phone station.
All Signallers advancing advance with 5th wave = B coy.
Lieut. MEEKING will be I/c A.R.C.

(b) Visual.
4 Signallers will establish a Visual station at CEMETERY working back to Batt. H.Q.
Bde Visual station near junction of YIDDISH ST & Y4&R
Each message will be sent twice.

(c) Runners.
4 per coy with O.C. coys.
2 " " of A.B.C. at A.R.C.
2 " " " at Batt H.Q.

Should telephonic communication break down between R.C and A.R.C the Officer I/c latter will send runners to hand in messages at R.C. until the break can be repaired.
R.C. will not be manned as a station, a clear line being left through from Batt H.Q. to A.R.C.
Similarly when Batt. H.Q. advances a clear line must be left through from Bde H.Q. to A.R.C.

(d) CTs
A new CT will be dug under Div. arrangements from YELLOW ST to EMS. YELLOW ST – EMS CT will be used for UP traffic only.
Q.W.R. are allotted exclusive use of ETCH.
The first opportunity will be taken to remove one wire from the lines laid forward from R.C. & to place it in the new CT.

Flares. Red flares will be placed on the objective trenches as soon as reached. O.C coys will detail men to do this.
Boards. Coys will carry boards on which the names of their objective trenches are painted. These boards will be placed at centre of fire trenches & at W. end of CTs on arrival.

12. Distinguishing Colours.

A will wear Red Tape on right shoulder strap
B " " Blue " " " " "
C " " Black " " " " "
D " " Yellow " " " " "
All wire cutters } White " " " " " in addition
Company colours
Signallers . Blue & White

Right Coy of L.R.B wear Red on the left shoulder.
Other L.R.B coys   Blue
                    Yellow
                    Green.

13. Consolidation and Work in Trenches

As soon as objective trenches are reached by A.B.C. no time must be wasted to commence work of consolidation. The first hour will no doubt be the quietest, & every man must do his utmost to make good & strengthen the trenches against counter attack.

Frequent progress reports to be sent to C.O. via A.R.S.

14. Clearing GOMMECOURT PARK & village.

2 hours after Zero time GOMMECOURT PARK & village are to be cleared by L.R.B & Q.V.R respectively.

Small Bombing parties will be formed from Hd. B. D coys under Lt CALEY. The village of GOMMECOURT will be systematically cleared from the STRONG POINT & CEMETERY in a N.W direction, as far as the pond S. of Church & S.W as far as FIBRE & to get into touch with L.R.B clearing the PARK. Progress to be reported to A.R.S.

15. Trench Mortars.

The ½ Section T.M.B. (2 mortars) will follow the 5th wave, and take up a suitable position about EMDEN to cover CEMETERY & STRONG POINT.

O.C. D will detail 10 men to report to O.C T.M.B. & they will carry STOKES ammunition for the day.

16. S.A.A. and Grenades.

Dumps as indicated in Administrative Instructions.
Every man will carry 120 rounds in equipment
                    100   "   2 bandoliers.

Batt. Reserve S.A.A will be situated at junction of YANKEE ST & Y47.L. This reserve will be sent forward to junction of FERN - FEVER on application from A.R.S.

Every man with exceptions specified in Q.V. 268/2 will carry 2 Bombs MILLS.

O.C coys will arrange for dumps of their grenades to be made on arrival at their objectives.

17. Dumps. Other than those mentioned in Q. administrative Instructions.

1. ½ man loads (50 - 60 of wiring material) behind Y.47. to right & left of YANKEE ST.
   25 ladders for carrying forward are in each of the portions of Y.47 occupied by A & C: 25 per coy.

   ½ man loads made up according to JOHNSAP is as under:—
   Screw pickets   2 per load
   Barbed wire   1 coil
   French wire   2 small coils & 6 staples
   X.P. metal   5 half sheets
   Planks. 4'   4
   Pickets wood. 5'   2
   Sandbags   40.

   The above is carried by B.

18. Battle Police.
   1 N.C.O. & 2 men with each section of Coy Bombers.
   Battle Police will wear 4" x 2" round right forearm.
   Duties:—
   (a) The B.P. must know what trench they are in, & be able to direct any man who is lost or doubtful where he is.
   (b) They must assist Bombers in clearing trenches and take charge of any prisoners, disarm them, & see that they are escorted back.
   (c) To see that no stragglers are left in the trenches behind those occupied by their coys; any so found they must send up to their coys.
   (d) To see that the C.S. are used correctly.

19. Bridges.
   50 Bridges (light), for carrying forward are in Y.47.   23 for A.
                                                            27 – C.
   A will bridge FEVER FEINT FELLOW.
   C „   „   FERN FEED EMDEN FEUD.
   To be done as quickly as possible to enable G.W.R. to pass over the QUADRILATERAL.

20. Smoke Arrangements
   1. Smoke will be freely used whatever the direction of the wind.
   2. Smoke will be propelled from (a) 4" STOKES mortars under arrangements by O.C. 5th Spec. Bde. R.E. (b) by hand, by 167 Bde.
   3. On day of attack (a) Spec. Bde will have 6 Mortars for left smoke Barrage on F.1.R. 12 Mortars along front between WHISKEY & Z hedge, to project smoke along the front.
   (b) Provided wind is favourable, smoke will be projected by hand along the whole Div. front from HÉBUTERNE – PUISIEUX road to the Sap head at K.3.d.4.7.

The intention is that the assault should start as soon as possible after the commencement of the smoke, & that it should be kept up while the assaulting Batts are crossing No Mans Land, & that afterwards sufficient should be employed to screen parties working in C⁰ˢ across No Mans Land.

4. Smoke will be used freely during the preliminary bombardment.

5. Lines of chloride of lime will be laid at different points in the Southern part of No Mans Land shewing the true direction of advance.

All ranks should look out for these lines, & correct their direction by them.

<u>Battalion HQ.</u> will be at junction of YELLOW s⁺ & Y 47 R.
later at or near A.R.C.

J. Chudmur
Capt & Adj⁺
Q.V.R.

27.6.16.

APPENDIX showing Tools etc carried.

Wire cutters (large & small)
Wire meshes.
Billhooks.
Periscopes (Wigstead Box)
Sandbags
Grenades
Shovels
Picks.

	Q	R	S	T	U	V	W	X	Y	Z
A	35	15	90	10	140	3	500	360	40	10
B		20	20	18		2	600	360	115	40
C	35	15	90	10	140	4	600	360	60	30
D	10	40	60					380		
L.G						3	95		16	10
HQ Bombers						2	50		10	
Sigs.							30		4	

169th Brigade.

56th Division.

1/9th BATTALION

LONDON REGIMENT

JULY 1916

Army Form C. 2118.

169 J6

Vol 20

WAR DIARY
9th Battn London Regt or Queen Victoria's Rifles
INTELLIGENCE SUMMARY.
(Erase heading not required.)

Instructions regarding War Diaries and Intelligence Summaries are contained in F.S. Regs., Part II. and the Staff Manual respectively. Title pages will be prepared in manuscript.

Place	Date	Hour	Summary of Events and Information	Remarks and references to Appendices
(ST AMAND) HEBUTERNE	1916 JULY 1		Battalion left billets in ST AMAND 8·0 - 9·30 pm. 30.6.16 and took up position in assembly trenches, Y sector. Attack carried out as per summary rendered last month. Casualties: Killed Officers 6 O.Rks 51; Wounded 5 290; Missing 5 188; Total 16 529	MAP 1/100000 LENS sheet 11. (H) (5)
BAYENCOURT	2		Battalion relieved by 12th London Regt + withdrew to billets in BAYENCOURT	— (5)
ST AMAND	3		Battalion withdrew to billets in ST AMAND arriving 4·0 pm.	
	4		Draft arrived - 80 O.Rks y/t midnhe. 80 O.Rks. 8th midnhe.	
	5			
FONQUEVILLERS	6		Battalion marched from ST AMAND (leaving 3·30-4·15 pm) to FONQUEVILLERS relieving 14th London Regt (London Scottish). Hd Qrs. + 1 Company in reserve dugouts - 2 companies in trenches, Z sector. (Battalion formed into 3 Companies.	— (5) (H)
	7		Clearing and improvement of trenches.	

M.P.A.Dickins Lieut-Col
O.C. Queen Victoria's Rifles

WAR DIARY
or
INTELLIGENCE SUMMARY.

(Erase heading not required.)

Army Form C. 2118.

Place	Date	Hour	Summary of Events and Information	Remarks and references to Appendices
	1916 JULY			
FONQUEVILLERS	8		Battalion in Trenches and reserve dugouts.	
	9		Cleaning and improving trenches	
	10			
	11			
	12		Battalion relieved by 8th Middlesex & 3rd London Regts., and moved to Billets in FONQUEVILLERS.	
	13		Draft arrived - 83 O.Rks. 20th London Regt.	
	14		R.E. Fatigues. Battalion marched to HANNESCAMP relieving 8/Somerset L.I. H.Q. and 3 platoons in reserve dug outs. 2 companies 1 platoon in trenches. 1 Company in Support.	
HANNESCAMP	15			LENS II (H) (5)
	16		A drafts arrived - 1st Lond. 6 O.Rks., 3rd Lond. 15 O.Rks., 4th Lond. 8 O.Rks., 8th Lond. 189 O.Rks. 13th Lond. 10 O.Rks., 14th Lond. 24 O.Rks.	
	17		Cleaning and improving trenches.	
	18			
	19		Battalion relieved by 5th Lond. Regt. (L.R.B) Hd. Qrs. & 3 Companies marched to billets in FONQUEVILLERS.	
			BIENVILLERS. 1 Company to billets in FONQUEVILLERS.	

W.R. Pickins Lieut-Col.
O.C. Queen Victorias Rifles

WAR DIARY
or
INTELLIGENCE SUMMARY.

(Erase heading not required.)

Army Form C. 2118.

Instructions regarding War Diaries and Intelligence Summaries are contained in F. S. Regs., Part II. and the Staff Manual respectively. Title pages will be prepared in manuscript.

Place	Date	Hour	Summary of Events and Information	Casualties		Remarks and references to Appendices
				Officers	O. Ranks	
BIENVILLERS	1916 JULY 20		R.E. fatigues digging and cleaning communication trenches.		5 Killed 11 Wded.	Fatigue Party shelled.
FONQUEVILLERS	21		Billets in BIENVILLERS shelled.		4 Killed 8 Wded.	
	22		Battalion relieved by 5th Lond Regt. & proceeded to FONQUEVILLERS relieving 16th Lond Regt. 3 Companies less 1 platoon in trenches, Z Sector. Hd. Qrs. and remainder of Battn. in dugouts.			
	23				1 Killed 4 Wded.	
	24					
	25		O.Rkrs. of 1st, 3rd, H.4, 13th, 114th Lond. Regts. attchd. B.V.R. transferred to own units.		4 Killed 8 Wded.	
	26				1 Wded	
	27					
	28		Trenches cleared & repaired. Stores & equipment salved.			
	29					
	30		Battalion relieved by 16th London Regt. & marched to billets in ST AMAND			
ST. AMAND	31					

Hopkins Lieut-Col.
O.C. Queen Victorias Rifles

WAR DIARY or INTELLIGENCE SUMMARY.

9th Battn London Regt Queen Victoria's Rifles

Report on Operations at GOMMECOURT 1st July 1916

On the night of June 30/July 1 the Battalion moved up into its position of assembly as follows:—

"A" & "C" Companies in Y.47 and the BOYAU de SERVICE Attached to "C" Company were 1 platoon 5th Cheshires and 8 R.E.

"B" Company in Y.47.L with ½ Section 169th Trench Mortar Battery.

"D" Company in Y.47.R in reserve

Battalion H.Q. at the junction of YELLOW STREET and Y.47.R

The objective of the Battalion was as follows:—

"A" Coy through FEVER FEINT FELLOW FELL & EPTE (exclusive)

"B"   "   FERN EMS (inclusive) FEED EMDEN to FEUD STRONG POINT & CEMETERY. As soon as STRONG POINT was established and EMS was clear 1 platoon of "B" Coy in FEUD was to re-inforce EMS getting into touch with Q.W.R. at QUADRILATERAL. The platoon of "A" Coy in FELLOW & FELL were then to move to their left and be in support in FEUD & FELLOW.

Army Form C. 2118.

WAR DIARY
or
INTELLIGENCE SUMMARY.
(Erase heading not required.)

Place	Date	Hour	Summary of Events and Information	Remarks and references to Appendices
			"B" Coy through FEVER FERR to FEINT FEED. A further phase to commence 3 hours after the time of the assault consisted in bombing parties from H.Q. bombers and "B" & "D" Companies clearing GOMMECOURT PARK and VILLAGE. These parties were to clear from STRONG POINT and CEMETERY as far as the pond S. of the Church and S.W. as far as FIBRE and get into touch with L.R.B.	
		6.25 a.m.	Intensive bombardment of enemy's line began.	
		7.20 a.m.	Smoke began (four minutes too soon) from the Z hedge and at	
		7.25 "	Smoke was issued all along the line and the first two companies moved forward.	
		7.30 "	The Assault commenced, the artillery lifting off the enemy's first line of trenches. The Assault was carried out in a series of waves as follows:— 1st wave 1 Platoon each of "A" & "C" at 4 paces interval. 2nd " 2 " " " " " " " " 3rd " 1 " " " " " " " " 4th " 3 Sections H.Q. Bombers, 1 Platoon Cheshires, 8 Sappers.	

Army Form C. 2118.

WAR DIARY
or
INTELLIGENCE SUMMARY.
(Erase heading not required.)

Place	Date	Hour	Summary of Events and Information	Remarks and references to Appendices
		5 am	"B" Company at 2 paces interval 1/2 Section T.M.B. Signallers.	
			As soon as the assault commenced the German Barrage was opened on to our trenches, though not severe at first it increased in intensity later.	
		9.48 am	By 9.48 am the assaulting companies had reached their objective and occupied FEUD FELLOWS FELL after heavy fighting. They did not however get in touch at EPTE with the Battalion on the right (the left Battalion of the Brigade on the right). At the same time the Third Company was consolidating the German 2nd line. The Germans were pressing hard at this time and the shortage of Bombs began to be felt.	
		10.30 am	In accordance with the orders reets the 4th phase 3 Sections of Bombers with battle police from the Reserve Company were ordered at 9.30 am to join the Companies in the German line. Owing to the congestion in Y & Y R and the communication trenches this party did not leave BHQ after 10.30. As soon as the party left the trench they came under heavy machine gun fire and half	

WAR DIARY
or
INTELLIGENCE SUMMARY.

(Erase heading not required.)

Army Form C. 2118.

Place	Date	Hour	Summary of Events and Information	Remarks and references to Appendices
		11.0 a.m.	the party found casualties immediately. This party was unable to get across No mans land the enemy's barrage by this time being intense. Shortage of bombs became critical.	
		12.30 pm to 1.30 pm	German counter attack increased in force and the companies were driven back from the 3rd line to the 2nd line.	
		2.0 pm	Companies driven back to German 1st line. About this time a few wounded men began to reach our lines. The Battalion was ordered to collect all stragglers in our lines and hold Y. 44 strongly.	
		4.30 pm	From this time up to about 4.0 pm survivors in German trenches kept up the resistance but at 4.0 pm they were finally driven out and those who got across No mans Land began to return to our trenches.	
		7.0 pm	After dark the Battalion took up the position in Y.44.c & Y.44 R. and remained there for the night and the next day until the afternoon when it withdrew to BAYENCOURT.	

W.P. Atkins Lt Col
O.C. Queen Victoria's Rifles

169th Brigade.
56th Division.

1/9th BATTALION

LONDON REGIMENT (Q.V.R.)

AUGUST 1916

Army Form C. 2118.

1/9th Battn. London Regt. or Queen Victoria Rifles

WAR DIARY
INTELLIGENCE SUMMARY.
(Erase heading not required.)

Instructions regarding War Diaries and Intelligence Summaries are contained in F.S. Regs. Part II. and the Staff Manual respectively. Title pages will be prepared in manuscript.

Place	Date	Hour	Summary of Events and Information	Casualties Offs. / O.Rks.	Remarks and references to Appendices
ST. AMAND	1916 AUG. 1		Battalion in Billets. Company training. Training of Lewis Gunners, Bombers and Patrol Party. R.E. fatigues.		MAP 1/100,000 LENS 11 (3)
	2				
	3				
	4		Battalion inspected by Brigadier General Commanding 169th Inf. Bde. and Burnt Cards presented to 4 Other Ranks for Meritorious Service 1.7.16.		
	5				
	6				
FONQUEVILLERS	7		Battalion marched to FONQUEVILLERS, relieving 16th London Regt. 3 Companies, less 1 platoon in trenches Z 54-61. Hd. Qrs. remainder of Battalion in Augonvz.	1 Wounded 1 .	(4) (5)
	8		} Trenches cleaned and repaired. Wire strengthened. Augonvz huts.	1 Wounded	
	9				
	10				
	11				
	12				

V.W.P.Bishop Lieut. Col.
C.O. Queen Victoria Rifles

WAR DIARY
or
INTELLIGENCE SUMMARY.

(Erase heading not required.)

Army Form C. 2118.

Place	Date	Hour	Summary of Events and Information	Casualties		Remarks and references to Appendices
				Offs.	O. Rks.	
FONQUEVILLERS	1916 AUG 13		Battalion in Trenches Z 54-61 and Dugouts			
	14		Battalion relieved by 16th London Regt - HQ 4rs & 3 Companies moved to billets in BIENVILLERS, 1 Company remaining in dugouts FONQUEVILLERS		1 Wounded.	
do "	15					
BIENVILLERS	16					
	17					
	18		Battalion marched from BIENVILLERS (leaving 11.0 pm) & billets in BEAUDRICOURT (arriving 1.30 am)			
BEAUDRICOURT	19		} Company training			LENS 11 (E) (4)
	20					
	21					
VILLERS L'HOPITAL	22		Battalion marched from BEAUDRICOURT (leaving 6.45 am) & billets at VILLERS L'HOPITAL (arriving 12.30 pm)			(E) (4)
ARGENVILLERS	23		Battalion marched from VILLERS L'HOPITAL (leaving 6.25 am) to billets at ARGENVILLERS (arriving 4.0 pm)			ABBEVILLE (L) (4)

Hugh Brooking Lieut-Col.
O.C. Queen Victoria's Rifles

Army Form C. 2118.

WAR DIARY
or
INTELLIGENCE SUMMARY.
(Erase heading not required.)

Instructions regarding War Diaries and Intelligence Summaries are contained in F. S. Regs., Part II. and the Staff Manual respectively. Title pages will be prepared in manuscript.

Place	Date	Hour	Summary of Events and Information	Remarks and references to Appendices
ARGENVILLERS	1916 Aug 24			
	25		Comprehensive programme of training for Companies and all details carried out, including Battalion attack practice	
	26			
	27			
	28			
	29			
	30			
	31			

W.P.Pickard Lieut-Col
O.C. Queen Victoria Rifles

169th Brigade.
56th Division.

1/9th BATTALION

LONDON REGIMENT

SEPTEMBER 1916.

WAR DIARY or INTELLIGENCE SUMMARY.

Army Form C. 2118.

(Erase heading not required.)

Instructions regarding War Diaries and Intelligence Summaries are contained in F.S. Regs., Part II and the Staff Manual respectively. Title pages will be prepared in manuscript.

1/4 London R.B. Vol 2

Place	Date	Hour	Summary of Events and Information	Remarks and references to Appendices
ARBENVILLERS	1916 Sept. 1		Battalion in Billets. Company training. Evening B Luini Dinners. Bon hire etc	MAP/100000 AMIENS 17
	2			
CORBIE	3		Batts marched to ST RIQUIER entraining Chinese for CORBIE	
	4		Batts marched from CORBIE (leaving 2pm) to Camp in HAPPY VALLEY near BRAY.	
	5		Batts in Camp	
	6		Batts moved up to CASEMENT trench between MARICOURT & MONTAUBON	
	7		" " took over trenches from 1st London Rgt in LEUZE WOOD.	
	8			
	9		Batts assaulted and captured trench 300 yds E of LEUZE WOOD and of BW end of BOULEAUX WOOD. This trench was named VICTORIA TRENCH & subsequently renamed BULLY TRENCH.	MAP FRANCE 57d SW
	10		Captured position maintained. Battn relieved by 13th Composite Brigade at 11.0pm & withdrew to CITADEL FRICOURT.	
	11			
	12		Battn marched from CITADEL to point near BILLON WOOD	
	13		Battn relieved 13th Composite Brigade & took over LEUZE MEERE trench.	

Army Form C. 2118.

WAR DIARY
or
INTELLIGENCE SUMMARY.
(Erase heading not required.)

Instructions regarding War Diaries and Intelligence Summaries are contained in F. S. Regs., Part II. and the Staff Manual respectively. Title pages will be prepared in manuscript.

Place	Date	Hour	Summary of Events and Information	Remarks and references to Appendices
	1916 Sep.			
	14		Battn in LEUZE WOOD Trench.	
	15		Battn formed defensive flank for XIV offensive operations. Draft of 49 O.Ranks arrived.	
	16			
	17		Draft of 196 O.Ranks arrived. Battn in trenches i.e. LOOP. FUSILIERS. CHESHIRE & COMBLES TRENCHES.	
	18			
	19		Draft of 38 O.Ranks arrived.	
	20		Battn relieved in front line by 2nd LONDON Regt & went into FALFEMONT FARM line.	
	21			
	22			
	23		Battn relieved 5th London Regt in trenches S.E. of LEUZE WOOD.	
	24		At 5.30 am Grenade assault was made on COMBLES TRENCH & was repulsed. Battn was relieved by 5th London Regt and went into Brigade Reserve in FALFEMONT FARM line.	

2353 Wt. W2544/1454 700,000 5/15 D.D.&L. A.D.S.S./Forms/C. 2118.

Army Form C. 2118.

WAR DIARY
or
INTELLIGENCE SUMMARY.
(Erase heading not required.)

Place	Date	Hour	Summary of Events and Information	Remarks and references to Appendices
	1916 SEPT			
	25		XIV Corps offensive renewed.	
	26		Battn. stood by ready to enter COMBLES, evacuated by the enemy. Battn. relieved at 4.0 pm by 167th Brigade & withdrawn to CASEMENT Trenches.	
	27		Battn. moved into billets at MEAULTE.	
	28			
	29		Battn. moved into CRATERS near GERMAN WOOD.	
	30		Battn. relieved 2nd Sherwood Foresters in LESBOEUFS SECTOR.B line.	

Signed,
Capt. a/Adjt.
for O.C Queen Victoria Rifles

56

1/9 London Regt.

Vol XVII

1/9th Bn. London Regt. WAR DIARY or Queen Victoria Rifles
INTELLIGENCE SUMMARY
Army Form C. 2118.

Vol 23

Place	Date	Hour	Summary of Events and Information	Remarks and references to Appendices
CARNOY / LES BOEUFS	1916 Oct 1		Battalion in trenches - LES BOEUFS Sectr. Patrol sent out under 2/Lt GUTTERIDGE under cover of barrage fire, but met with no success. 2/Lt GUTTERIDGE missing. Front and Support lines heavily shelled. Battalion relieved by 1/5th Lond. (L.R.B.) at 11.0 p.m. & withdrew to HOG'S BACK trench in support.	MAP 1/40000 ALBERT T. 3
	2			
	3		Battalion withdrew 5.0 p.m. to CITADEL, FRICOURT, but progress considerably delayed by heavy hostile shelling & bad state of roads. Battn. reached Camp at 12.0 midnight.	F. 3.
FRICOURT	4		Battalion in Camp	
	5			
	6			
	7		Battalion moved up at 4.15 a.m. into Divnl. Reserve, S.E. of GINCHY and 4.15 p.m. moved up to HOG'S BACK trench to support 4th Lond. Regt. At 1.0 a.m. Battn. relieved 4th Londons & 12th Londons (Rangers) in FOGGY & BERNABY trenches. At 3.30 p.m. Battn. attacked GREEN line but were driven back at dusk to original line held by them.	S. 29
	8			
	9		Battalion relieved by 1/Bn. Royal Irish Fusiliers at 10.30 p.m. & withdrew to BERNAFAY Wood.	

V.W.F. Dickins Lieut-Col.
O.C. Queen Victorias Rifles

Army Form C. 2118.

WAR DIARY
or
INTELLIGENCE SUMMARY.

(Erase heading not required.)

Instructions regarding War Diaries and Intelligence Summaries are contained in F. S. Regs., Part II. and the Staff Manual respectively. Title pages will be prepared in manuscript.

Place	Date	Hour	Summary of Events and Information	Remarks and references to Appendices
FRICOURT	1916 Oct 10		Battalion withdrew to MANSELL CAMP, FRICOURT	ALBERT T.C.
	11		Battalion in Camp	
PICQUIGNY	12		Battalion marched from MANSELL Camp (leaving 5.0am) to TREUX whence they proceeded by Motor Buses to PICQUIGNY (arriving 1.0pm)	1/10/1916 AMIENS 17 (B) (1)
	13		⎫	
	14		⎜	
	15		⎜	
	16		⎬ Company training	
	17		⎜	
	18		⎜	
	19		⎜	
	20		⎭	
LIMEUX	21		Battalion marched from PICQUIGNY (leaving 8.0am) to billets in LIMEUX. (arriving 4.40pm)	(J) (6)
	22			
ST VENANT	23		Battalion marched from LIMEUX (leaving 10.0am) to PONT REMY where they entrained for BERGUETTE, they marched thence to billets in ST VENANT (arriving 12.30am 24th)	(K) (2) 14/10/1916 BETHUNE P.4.

J.W.P.B. Lieut. Col.
O.C. Queen Victoria's Rifles.

WAR DIARY
or
INTELLIGENCE SUMMARY

Army Form C. 2118.

Place	Date	Hour	Summary of Events and Information	Remarks and references to Appendices
	1916 Oct			1/40,000 BETHUNE
LESTREM	24		Battalion marched from ST VENANT (leaving 11.30 am) to billets in LESTREM (arriving 2.20 pm)	R.9.
	25		Company training	
	26		Company training	
	27		Battalion marched from LESTREM (leaving 8.40 am) to reserve billets in BOUT DEVILLE (arriving 11.0 am) relieving 2/6th Br. Gloucester.	R.24.
BOUT DEVILLE	28		Battalion relieved 2/4th Gloucesters in trenches in the NEUVE CHAPELLE Section	
	29		Battn. in trenches. Trenches cleared & drained.	
	30			
	31			

M.P.S. [signature] Lieut.-Col.
for OC Queen Victoria's Rifles

Narrative of Operations in LESBOEUFS SECTOR,

from 7th. - 10th. October, 1916.

*by 168 Inf. Bde were received at 7.15 pm

At 7.15 a.m. on October 7th. the Q.V.R. moved from rest Camp at CITADEL to trenches N.E. of GUINCHY to take up their position in Divisional Reserve. The Battalion, moving by cross-country tracks were in position by 11 a.m. As the Q.V.R. was the most forward Battalion of a Brigade in Divisional Reserve a sudden move was anticipated. Orders issued at 5.30 p.m.* directing the Q.V.R. to move forthwith to HOGSBACK TRENCH in squares T.3.d., T.1.c., and T.2.d. with H.Q. at T.2.d.8.9. This move was complete at 8.30 p.m. although the trenches referred to were found on arrival to be already occupied by 2 Companies of KENSINGTONS and some details of 3rd. London Regt.

Orders from 169th. Infantry Brigade informed the Q.V.R. that they were at the disposal of the 168th. Infantry Brigade. From what information there was it appeared that the 168th. Infantry Brigade had been counter-attacked at dusk and forced back to their original position. Q.V.R. shared their H.Q. with 4th. Londons. At 11 p.m. a message was received by telephone from 168th. Infantry Brigade ordering two Companies of the Q.V.R. to relieve 2 Companies of 4th. London Regt. in POPPY TRENCH. "C" and "B" Companies were thereupon detailed to carry out this relief. This order was shortly followed by another to the effect that the remaining 2 Companies of Q.V.R. should relieve 2 Companies of RANGERS in BURNABY and BURNABY SUPPORT TRENCHES. "D" Company Q.V.R. was ordered to relieve BURNABY and "A" Company BURNABY SUPPORT TRENCH.

At 12.30 a.m. a conference was held with Company Commanders concerning future operations which involved the assault of the GREEN LINE by Q.V.R. at 3.30 p.m. on the 8/10/16. At this hour the D.W.R. would assault RAINY TRENCH. The dividing line between Q.V.R. and D.W.R. was through T.4.b.9.2. - T.5.a.3.5. - N.35.c.5.0. The Company objectives of the Q.V.R. were allotted as follows:-

(i) "D" Company to capture GUN EMPLACEMENTS and GUN PITS in T.5.a.3.7. and thence to a front about 225 yards at N.35.c.7.0. on a frontage of 200 yards.
(ii) "C" Company to advance on the left of "D" and to establish itself for 200 yards N.W. of left of "D".
(iii) "B" Company to clear RAINY TRENCH which should be empty - capture DUNLOP and then advance 225 yards to N.35.c.2.3. and get in touch with 167th. Inf. Bde on the left.
(iv) "A" Company to remain in reserve.

On attaining their objectives Companies were ordered to dig in and consolidate.

At 4.a.m. "C" and & "B" Companies were reported to have arrived in POPPY TRENCH. At 4.30 a.m. "D" Company reported the relief of the RANGERS in BURNABY TRENCH complete. About this time "A" Company who were to relieve the RANGERS in BURNABY SUPPORT TRENCH returned to Battalion H.Q. and reported that there were no guides to meet them in LESBOEUFS as has been previously arranged.

Two Platoons were thereupon sent back to LESBOEUFS with orders to obtain guides from RANGERS H.Q. These two Platoons eventually established themselves in THISTLE TRENCH. The other two Platoons were detained at Battalion H.Q. for carrying purposes.

The three assaulting Companies in the front line reported that there were very few picks and shovels, no bombs and no reserve ammunition in their lines. Accordingly all available H.Q. details and the two Platoon of "A" Company were employed in carrying bombs, ammunition and tools from the various dumps to the front line. This work was done in broad daylight and over open ground. It soon became clear that it was quite impossible for any of these stores to reach "B" Company as daylight communication between BURNABY TRENCH and Q.V.R. H.Q. was practically cut off.

By 11.30 a.m. "D","C","B" Companies were reported in position for the attack. Owing to the heavy hostile bombardment of the front and support trenches it was impossible to send sufficient bombs, ammunition and tools to the assaulting Companies. At 1 p.m. orders were received from the Division that in spite of an adverse situation the attack was to be carried out at 2.30 p.m.

At this hour an intense barrage was opened on the enemy's lines and shortly afterwards it was reported from the advanced report centre that the attack was going well. The positions attained, however, were not sufficiently strongly held to be maintained and shortly after dusk the Q.V.R. were forced back to their original lines. This line was held until handed over to the 1st. Bn. Royal Irish Fusiliers at 8 P.m. the following day.

On 15/10/16 the battalion marched from BERNAFAY WOOD to MANSELLCAMP and proceeded thence on the 18th. inst. to PICQUIGNY where they again came under the orders of the 169th. Infantry Bde.

Sd. Nicholl, Capt. & Adjt.
for O.C. Queen Victoria Rifles.

14/10/16.

Somme Operations

Army Form C. 2118.

WAR DIARY
1/9th Bn. London Regt. Queen Victoria's Rifles
or
INTELLIGENCE SUMMARY.

(Erase heading not required.)

Vol 24

Place	Date	Hour	Summary of Events and Information	Remarks and references to Appendices
NEUVE CHAPELLE	1916 Nov. 1		Battalion in trenches. Trenches repaired & drained.	MAP 1/40,000 BETHUNE M.35
	2		Battalion relieved by 16th London Regt. & proceeded to billets in BOUT DEVILLE	R.24
BOUT DEVILLE	3			
	4		Battalion carried out Company training & practice in anti-gas measures. Training of details.	
	5			
	6			
	7			
	8			
NEUVE CHAPELLE	9		Battalion relieved 16th London Regt. in trenches.	
	10			
	11		Battalion in trenches	
	12			
	13			
	14			
CROIX BARBEE	15		Battalion relieved by 16th London Regt. & proceeded to CROIX BARBEE, 3 Companies in billets, 1 Company holding defensive posts.	M.26

R. M. Lindsay-Rae Major
O.C. Queen Victoria's Rifles.

Army Form C. 2118.

WAR DIARY
or
INTELLIGENCE SUMMARY.
(Erase heading not required.)

Instructions regarding War Diaries and Intelligence Summaries are contained in F. S. Regs., Part II. and the Staff Manual respectively. Title pages will be prepared in manuscript.

Place	Date	Hour	Summary of Events and Information	Remarks and references to Appendices
CROIX BARBEE	1916 Nov. 16		Battalion in billets & holding defensive posts.	
	17			
	18		R.E. and carrying fatigues.	
	19			
	20			
NEUVE CHAPELLE	21		Battalion relieved 16th London Regt. in trenches.	
	22			
	23		12.45 a.m. Bangalore Torpedo successfully exploded under enemy wire at M.35.a.8.1.	
	24			
	25			
	26		2 Coys: 2½ Companies relieved by 4th Bn. Middx. Northothrens at RIEZ BAILLEUL. ½ Coy. closing up in "B" line.	
LA GORGUE	27		1½ Companies relieved by 16th Bn. Royal Warwicks. Whole Battn. proceeded to billets in LA GORGUE	Sheet 36 A 1/40000 L.34.
	28			
	29		Company training in all branches.	
	30			

R.J. Lindsey-Renton Major
O.C. Queen Victorias Rifles

1/9th Bn. London Regt. WAR DIARY Queen Victoria's Rifles Army Form C. 2118.
or
INTELLIGENCE SUMMARY.

Vol 25

Place	Date	Hour	Summary of Events and Information	Remarks and references to Appendices
LA GORGUE	1916 DEC 1		Battalion in Billets	Map 1/40000 Sheet 36A L.34.
	2			
	3		Company Training. Training of Lewis Gunners & Bombers.	
	4		R.E. Fatigues	
	5			
	6			
	7		Battalion inspected by XI Corps Commander.	
	8			
NEUVE CHAPELLE	9		Battalion proceeded to Trenches & relieved 3rd Bn. London Regt. in NEUVE CHAPELLE Sector.	" M.26.
	10		Battalion in Trenches	
	11			
	12			
	13			
	14			
PONT DU HEM	15		Battalion relieved by 16th Lond. Regt. (Q.W.R.) - Hd.Qrs. & 3 Coys. proceeded to Billets in PONT DU HEM. 1 Coy. holding defensive posts at ROUGE CROIX	1/40,000 Sheet 36 M.21 & M.24.

R.H. Luson Major
O.C. Queen Victoria's Rifles

Army Form C. 2118.

WAR DIARY
or
INTELLIGENCE SUMMARY.
(Erase heading not required.)

Instructions regarding War Diaries and Intelligence Summaries are contained in F. S. Regs., Part II. and the Staff Manual respectively. Title pages will be prepared in manuscript.

Place	Date	Hour	Summary of Events and Information	Remarks and references to Appendices
	1916			
PONT DU HEM & ROUGE CROIX	DEC 16			
	17		R.E. Fatigues. Training of Bombers.	
	18			
	19			
	20			
NEUVE CHAPELLE	21		Battalion relieved 16th Lond. Regt. (Q.W.R) in trenches	
	22			
	23		Section of front line trench near MAUQUISSART Crater, after being shelled for 2 nights by hostile "minnies", was entered by enemy at 12.30 a.m. 23rd Decr who took 2 prisoners and caused 2 other casualties. Enemy returned to own lines under cover of renewed bombardment, after a stay of a few minutes in own trench.	
PONT DU HEM	24		Battalion relieved by 16th London Regt. (Q.W.R) & proceeded to PONT DU HEM & ROUGE CROIX	
	25			
	26			
	27		R.E. Fatigues	
	28			

R.J. Lindsay Pratt Major
O.C. Queen Victorias Rifles

Army Form C. 2118.

WAR DIARY
or
INTELLIGENCE SUMMARY.
(Erase heading not required.)

Instructions regarding War Diaries and Intelligence Summaries are contained in F. S. Regs., Part II. and the Staff Manual respectively. Title pages will be prepared in manuscript.

Place	Date	Hour	Summary of Events and Information	Remarks and references to Appendices
PONT DU HEM	1916 DEC 29		⎱ Working parties in trenches	
	30		⎰	
	31			

R.M. Lidger Rand — Major
O.O. Queen Victorias Rifles

Army Form C. 2118.

WAR DIARY
or
INTELLIGENCE SUMMARY.

1/9th Bn. London Regt. Queen Victorias Rifles

(Erase heading not required.)

Place	Date	Hour	Summary of Events and Information	Remarks and references to Appendices
PONT DU HEM	1916 JAN 1	19")	Working parties in trenches. Battn. in Billets	MAP 1/40,000 Sheet 36.M.21&27
ROBERMETZ	2		Battn. relieved by 12th Bn. London Regt. moved into Divisional Reserve at ROBERMETZ	MAP 1/40,000 K.24.
	3			
	4			
	5		Company and Specialist training in all branches	
	6			
	7			
	8		Working parties	
	9			
	10			
	11			
	12			
	13			
LAVENTIE	14		Battalion marched to LAVENTIE relieving 5th London Regt.	
	15		Working parties. Company training	
	16			

F. B. Follett Lieut-Col.
O.C. Queen Victorias Rifles.

Army Form C. 2118.

WAR DIARY or INTELLIGENCE SUMMARY.

1/9th Bn. London Regt. Queen Victoria's Rifles.

(Erase heading not required.)

Place	Date	Hour	Summary of Events and Information	Remarks and references to Appendices
LAVENTIE	1916 JAN. 14		Working parties. Company training	MAP 1/10000 AUBERS 36 SW. N.8 central & 15 central
	18			
	19			
	20		Battn. relieved 2nd. Bn. London Regt. in trenches FAUQUISSART Sector.	
	21		Battalion in trenches holding Posts in old German front line.	
	22		Posts heavily shelled and 1 Post raided by enemy on this occasion.	
	23		Considerable loss caused to our garrison.	
	24			
	25			
	26		Battn. relieved by 2nd. Bn. London Regt. & withdrew to billets in LAVENTIE.	
	27			
	28			
	29		Working parties. Training & inspection of Companies.	
	30			
	31			

F. B. Follett Lieut. Col.
O.C. Queen Victoria's Rifles.

Army Form C. 2118.

1/9th Bn. London Regt. **WAR DIARY**
or
Queen Victoria's Rifles
INTELLIGENCE SUMMARY.
(Erase heading not required.)

Vol 27

Instructions regarding War Diaries and Intelligence Summaries are contained in F. S. Regs. Part II. and the Staff Manual respectively. Title pages will be prepared in manuscript.

Place	Date	Hour	Summary of Events and Information	Remarks and references to Appendices
				MAPS/OPS AUBERS 36 SW1 N. & central & 13 central.
LAVENTIE	1914 FEB 1		Battalion relieved 2nd Bn. London Regt. in trenches, FAUQUISSART Sector	
	2			
	3		Battalion in trenches.	
	4			
	5			
	6			
	7		Battalion relieved by 2nd Bn. London Regt. & withdrew to billets in LAVENTIE	
	8			
	9		Working parties. Company training and training of Bombers, Lewis Gunners.	
	10			
	11			
	12			
	13			
	14		Battalion relieved 2nd Bn. London Regt. in trenches FAUQUISSART Sector	
	15		Battalion in trenches	
	16			

L. B. Follett Lieut-Col.
O.C. Queen Victoria's Rifles.

Army Form C. 2118.

WAR DIARY
or
INTELLIGENCE SUMMARY.
(Erase heading not required.)

Instructions regarding War Diaries and Intelligence Summaries are contained in F. S. Regs., Part II. and the Staff Manual respectively. Title pages will be prepared in manuscript.

Place	Date	Hour	Summary of Events and Information	Remarks and references to Appendices
LAVENTIE	1914 FEB 17		Battalion in Trenches	
	18			
	19		Battalion relieved by 2nd Bn. London Regt. with Hd.wk. billets in LAVENTIE	
	20			
	21		Working Parties. Company training. training of Bombers & Lewis Gunners	
	22			
	23			
	24			
	25		Battalion relieved 2nd Bn. London Regt. in trenches FACQUISSART Sector	
	26		Battalion in Trenches	
	27			
	28			

F. B. Hatt. Lieut-Col.
O.C. Queen Victoria Rifles

Army Form C. 2118.

1/9th Bn. London Regt. WAR DIARY Queen Victoria's Rifles
or
INTELLIGENCE SUMMARY.

Vol 28

(Erase heading not required.)

Instructions regarding War Diaries and Intelligence Summaries are contained in F. S. Regs., Part II. and the Staff Manual respectively. Title pages will be prepared in manuscript.

Place	Date	Hour	Summary of Events and Information	Remarks and references to Appendices
LA GORGUE	1914 MCH 1		Battalion relieved in trenches FAUQUISSART Sector, by 6th Bn. West Yorks Regt. & marched to billets in LA GORGUE.	
ST.FLORIS	2		Battalion marched from LA GORGUE to billets in ST FLORIS.	
	3		" " " " ST FLORIS . " SACHIN and PRESSY-LES-PERNES	
	4		" " " " SACHIN " WILLEMAN	
	5		" " " " WILLEMAN " REGNAUVILLE	
	6		" " " " REGNAUVILLE " ROUAEFAY	
	7		" " " " ROUAEFAY " IVERGNY	
	8		" " " " IVERGNY " GOUY-EN-ARTOIS	
GOUY-EN-ARTOIS	9		⎫	
	10		⎪	
	11		⎬ Company training in all branches.	
	12		⎪	
	13		⎭	
ARRAS	14		Battalion marched from GOUY-EN-ARTOIS to billets in ARRAS.	
	15			

L. B. Lott
Lieut-Col.
O.C. Queen Victoria's Rifles.

Army Form C. 2118.

WAR DIARY
or
INTELLIGENCE SUMMARY.
(Erase heading not required.)

Instructions regarding War Diaries and Intelligence Summaries are contained in F. S. Regs., Part II. and the Staff Manual respectively. Title pages will be prepared in manuscript.

Place	Date	Hour	Summary of Events and Information	Remarks and references to Appendices
ARRAS	1914 MCH. 16		Battalion engaged on digging and improving communication trench, at night.	Map Reference
	17		Company training in billets for short periods during day.	
	18		Battalion marched from ARRAS to billets in ACHICOURT.	1/10000 Sheet 57 S.S.W.1. M.L. a y 3
ACHICOURT	19		Battalion moved up into Support and Reserve trenches, relieved by 2nd London Regt.	
	20		Battalion relieved 2nd London Regt. in front line.	
	21			
	22		Positions evacuated by enemy consolidated.	M.78 y 24.
	23			
	24		Advanced posts established.	
	25			
	26		Batt. relieved by 2nd Lond. Regt. & 16th Lond. Regt. withdrew to billets in ACHICOURT.	
	27			
	28		Batt. engaged at night on digging assembly trenches for assault.	
	29			
	30		Batt. relieved 16th London Regt. in support trenches	M.10.
	31		Batt. in support trenches.	

F. B. Follett Lieut.-Col.
O.C. Queen Victoria's Rifles.

SECRET.

Headquarters,
56th Division.

B.M.447.

Reference B.M.445 of 2.4.17, War Diary for 9th London Regt. is now forwarded herewith.

E.S. D'A. Coke
Brig. Genl.
For Commdg. 169th Inf. Bde.

3rd May 1917.

Army Form C. 2118.

19th Bn. London Regt. Queen Victoria Rifles

WAR DIARY or INTELLIGENCE SUMMARY.

(Erase heading not required.)

Place	Date	Hour	Summary of Events and Information	Remarks and references to Appendices
MONCHIET	1919 APRIL 1		Battalion relieved by Unit of 168th Inf. Bde. in Reserve trenches in old British & German Front Line moved to rest billets in MONCHIET.	
	2			
	3			
	4			
	5			
	6		Training and Preparation for III Army Offensive Operations.	
	7		Battalion moved from MONCHIET at 6.0 p.m. to C.I. Area S.W. of AGNY. Transport and Q.M. Stores established at ACHICOURT.	
	8		Battalion ordered to be ready to support 169th Inf. Bde in Offensive Operations on Front. At 9 p.m. Battalion moved from C.I. Area to 169th Inf. Bde. Area No 4 East of AGNY. Operation Order in case of Battalion Offensive issued at 11 p.m. ACHICOURT heavily shelled from 11 a.m. to 5 p.m. and Q.M. Stores considerably damaged.	
	9	5.30 a.m.	VI Corps Offensive commenced	
		4.45 a.m.	5-6 Divns, 14th Divn. & 30th Divn. of VII Corps, attack launched.	
		9.30 a.m.	Battalion moved forward to system of trenches S. of BEAURAINS.	

Army Form C. 2118.

WAR DIARY or INTELLIGENCE SUMMARY.

1/9th Bn. London Regt. Queen Victoria Rifles.

(Erase heading not required.)

Instructions regarding War Diaries and Intelligence Summaries are contained in F. S. Regs., Part II. and the Staff Manual respectively. Title pages will be prepared in manuscript.

Place	Date	Hour	Summary of Events and Information	Remarks and references to Appendices
	1917 APRIL 9	2 pm	Battalion placed under orders of B.G.C. 164th Inf. Bde. for tactical purposes and ordered forward to 164th Inf. Bde. Forward Area in M.24 central. Advance made in artillery formation under Artillery fire of 4.2 calibre and gas shells. 2nd Lt. HALLIFAX wounded in Sunken Road.	
	10	12.40 a.m	B.G.C. 164th Inf. Bde. gave warning order that Battalion would attack from LION TRENCH with objective WANCOURT LINE at 12 noon. C.O. and Company Commanders went forward to reconnoitre position	
		3 am	Operation Orders for the attack issued.	
		10 am	Battalion moved forward to assembly trenches in LION LANE. Battn. H.Q. established in NEUVILLE VITASSE at 11.45 am	
		12 noon	Zero Hour. British Creeping Barrage commenced. R.V.R. and 1/st Middx. checked by enemy M.G. Post in LION LANE.	
		12.30 pm	'C' Coy cleared M.G. Post in LION LANE and commenced bombing up NEUVILLE VITASSE TRENCH and ZOO TRENCH. 2nd Lts. RALLS & JOHNSTONE wounded	
		2 pm	THE E.G.G. Captured. Four machine guns taken. 5 Officers & 63 O.R. of 31st R.I.R. taken prisoners.	

Army Form C. 2118.

1/6th Bn. London Rys. or Queen Victoria's Rifles.

WAR DIARY or INTELLIGENCE SUMMARY.

(Erase heading not required.)

Place	Date	Hour	Summary of Events and Information	Remarks and references to Appendices
	1917 APRIL 10	4 pm	Cavalry moved forward in direction of WANCOURT.	
		5.30 pm	Objective as far as junction of NEUVILLE VITASSE TRENCH and ZOO TRENCH secured. One section of 167 T.M.B. moved forward to assist "A" Coy.	
		4.30 am	Objective on WANCOURT LINE secured after bombing attack in conjunction with Lewis Guns by "A" and "B" Coys.	
	11	9 am	"B" Coy crossed WANCOURT LINE and commenced bombing down HENINEL and THAMES TRENCH.	
		11.30 am	"B" Coy under 2nd. Lt. H.T. HOW captured the COT.	
		12.45 pm	B.A.C. 167th Inf Bde. ordered attack to be pushed forward as far as COJEUL RIVER.	
		4.30 pm	Whole system of trenches as far as COJEUL RIVER S.W. of HENINEL informed.	
		5 pm	Captured trenches handed over to 30th Divn. Battalion in support in WANCOURT LINE System. Battn. returned to 167th Inf. Bde. command.	
	12		Battn. H.Q. moved forward to the E.G.G. at 12 noon.	
		5 pm	Orders to support 2nd Londons in attack on CHERISY on 13th inst. received.	
	13.	5.30 am	Battalion moved forward to support area S.W. of HENINEL. Battn. H.Q. established	

WAR DIARY or Intelligence Summary

1/9th Bn London Regt. Queen Victoria's Rifles.

Army Form C. 2118.

Place	Date	Hour	Summary of Events and Information	Remarks and references to Appendices
	1917 APRIL 13	in the COT.		
		2 p.m.	Attack postponed.	
		4.30 p.m.	Battalion ordered to relieve 2nd Londons in front line E. of HENINEL immediately after dusk. Enemy Barrage placed on Ridge N.E. of HENINEL.	
		9 p.m.	Battalion warned that VII Corps would resume Offensive Operations at dawn.	
		11 p.m.	Relief of 2nd Londons complete.	
		12 Midnight.	Operation Order for advance on CHERISY by 169th Inf. Bde. with Q.V.R. on Right. Q.W.R. on Left. issued.	
	14	5.30 a.m.	Attack on CHERISY launched under cover of creeping Barrage. Enemy barrage and heavy machine gun fire on British front line.	
		6 a.m.	Advance held up short of first objective. Heavy casualties in A.B.+D. Companies. 2nd Lt. H.J. HOW killed. British troops on left reported retiring. A Coy. compelled to tie out under enemy MG until dusk when they withdrew to original line. Posts established at N.36.a.9.4. and N.3b.A.4.5. Casualties on 14th 11 officers & approximately 350 O.Rks.	
		11 p.m.	Battalion relieved by 1st London Regt. & returned to the E.G.G.	
	15	3 p.m.	Battalion moved to BEAURAINS to Dugouts.	

Army Form C. 2118.

WAR DIARY
1/9th Bn. London Regt. or Queen Victoria's Rifles.
INTELLIGENCE SUMMARY.
(Erase heading not required.)

Place	Date	Hour	Summary of Events and Information	Remarks and references to Appendices
	1917 APRIL 16		On Outposts at BEAURAINS	
	17		" " "	
	18		Battalion moved by 'bus to SOUASTRE.	
	19		Battalion in billets at SOUASTRE.	
	20		" " "	
	21		" " "	
	22		" " "	
	23		" " "	
	24		Battalion marched to billets in WANQUETIN.	
	25		" " "	
	26		" to billets in BERNEVILLE.	
	27		" " "	
	28		" to trenches near AIRY CORNER.	
	29		Battalion took over front line E. of GUEMAPPE from 3rd and 1st London Rifles.	
	30		" in front line.	

F. B. Follett Lieut-Col.
O.C. Queen Victoria's Rifles.

J.N. 217.   O.C. " " Coy.

Admininstrative Instructions for move to Divnl. Reserve. (No. 1.)

1. The Battalion will move to reserve trenches near AGNY on April 6th.

2. Personnel to be left behind will move to GOUY-EN-ARTOIS on April 5th. as per separate instruction

3. On April 7th. Packs will be dumped by platoons in Transport Lines at ACHICOURT. Great Coats will be included in the packs.

4. Four Yellow and Black Artillery Flags have been issued to companies. These will be carried by one man in each platoon but will only actually be used in the attack. The Division on our right will carry Red & Yellow flags.

5. One hundred and seventy rounds per man will be carried on leaving MONCHIET except by Specialists as detailed in S.S.135. The extra 50 rounds will be issued to-day.

6. Each company will be issued with 20 shovels and 10 picks. Details will be notified later.

7. Sixteen Mills Cup Attachments will be issued per Company.

    Also

        25 Bucket Carriers per Company.

        10 Belt Bags per Company.

        15 Waistcoat Carriers per Company.

    The above will be issued to-day & to-morrow.

8. Wirecutters and Hedging Gloves will be issued as follows:-

    Wirecutters S.A. 13 each A. and B.

                    12 each to C. and D.

    Wirecutters 14 inch   10 to each Coy.

    Wirecutters Mk. V   12 to each Coy.

Hedging Gloves will be issued later.

Wirecutters shoudd as far as possible be stuck in the belt and attached to the shoulder strap with a string.

9. Officers Commanding Companies must not take Company Money into action.

10. Latrines. On arrival in assembly areas Latrines will be dug in slits or blind trenches and not in the main trenches or communication trenches.

5.4.17.   (Sd)— Capt & Adjt

Q.V.R. INSTRUCTIONS No 4.

1. <u>Information.</u>

In conjunction with the attack by the 1st Army, the 3rd Army is to break through the enemy's defences and advance on CAMBRAI.

The 7th Corps is to attack on the right of and simultaneouly with the 6th Corps.

2. <u>Objective and Method of Attack of 56th Division.</u>

The objective and method of attack of the 56th Division have been described in Q.V.R.Instructions No 3,d/5-4-17.

3. <u>The Programme of Attack will be as follows:-</u>
    (a) The assault will be delivered on "Z" day.
    (b) The preparatory bombardment of the enemy's defences will be carried out on "V" "W" "X" and "Y" days (owing to alteration in programme to-day is "W" day).
    (c) Programme on "Z" day.

<u>At Zero.</u> 6th Corps to assault.
<u>At Zero + 2 hours</u> - 14th Division will advance.
<u>At Zero + 2 hours 15 minutes</u> - Barrage for 56th Divn.will be put down 50yds short of the German front line as shewn on the barrage map, and our Infantry will leave the trenches.

The barrage will be lifted after one minute on to the front line whence it will lift at varying times according as the Infantry arrive within assaulting distance. It will then begin to creep

On reaching the BLUE LINE there will be a halt, after which 167th and 168th Infantry Brigades will assault the HINDENBURG LINE (COJEUL SWITCH) as below.

<u>At Zero + 6 hours 30 minutes</u> - The troops of the 167th Infantry Bde. detailed for the attack on the HINDENBURG (COJEUL SWITCH) LINE will cross the sunken road N.20.c.6.2.-N.20.a.1.6.and assault.

<u>At Zero + 6 hours 40 minutes</u> - The troops of the 168th Infantry Bde. detailed for the attack on the same objective will assault.

As soon as the Easternmost trench of the HINDENBURG LINE has been captured, the 56th Divnl.Artillery will form a protective barrier on a North and South line, lasting for 30 minutes, under cover of which the troops of the 167th Inf.Bde.detailed for the attack on the WANCOURT-FEUCHY LINE will advance close to the barrage.

The barrage will then move fotward at the rate of 100 yds in 2 minutes, gradually swinging round until it is square with the objective.

4. <u>Defensive Flank.</u>

The 168th Inf.Bde.is prepared to form a defensive flank facing North-East in the event of the enemy's line on the North not being broken.

This defensive flank will follow the line N.14.c.0.2.-N.13.d.6.3.-N.13.b.1.0.-N.13.a.8.2.-N.13.a.6.2.-thence the Northern boundary of the Divn., and will consist of a series of strong points.

5. <u>Strong Points for the BLUE LINE.</u>

As soon as the BLUE LINE has been captured, strong points are to be constructed at approximately the following points.

    167th Inf. Bde. Near the SUGAR FACTORY (N.19.d.)
                  N.19.b.8.2.(junction of the OVAL & NEUVILLE VITASSE Trench).

                N.20.a.55.40.
                N.20.a.35.00.
    168th Inf. Bde. N.20.a.30.65.(S.end of MOSS Trench).
                N.14.c.0.2.
                N.13.d.6.3.
                N.13.b.1.0.

6. <u>Strong Points in Advance of the BLUE LINE.</u>

As soon as the Easternmost trench of the HINDENBURG LINE (or COJEUL SWITCH) has been by the 167th Inf. Bde.& 168th Inf.Bde and during the advance of the troops of the former to the BROWN LINE, consolidation or the digging of a new trench is to be immediately commenced & Strong Points constructed as necessary. Similarly the BROWN LINE will be consolidated when captured.

7. <u>Reforming.</u>

As soon as WANCOURT has been captured by the 30th Divn. troops of 56th Divn.will be reformed, covered by outposts of the 167th Bde.on the BROWN LINE. The area of the 169th Inf. Bde.for reforming will be the ground between the following co-ordinates:-
    M.10.b.70.75.-M.18.b.25.95.-M.18.c.7.6.-M.24.b.30.85.-M.24.c.40.15
M.16.c.0.9.

8. **Contact Aeroplanes.**

Contact Aeroplanes will call by Klaxon Horn for flares to be lit by the leading troops as near as possible at the following hours;-

Zero plus 3 hours 30 minutes.
Zero " 7 " 30 " .
Zero " 11 " .

9. **"Z" Day and Zero Hour.**

"Z" day will be 9th April.
Zero hour will be communicated later.

(Sgd) J.NICHOLS, Capt. & Adjt.
Queen Victoria's Rifles.

6/4/17.

Q.V.R. INSTRUCTIONS No 6.

Reference.   51 B & 51 C.   First Edition.   1/40,000

1 Information.
The Battalion will move from MONCHIET on the 7th inst. to C.1 area.

2 Move
Lewis Gun sections with their four Lewis Gun limbers will be facing East on the MONCHIET-BEAUMETZ Road ready to move at 6 p.m.; rear of sections to be clear of the fork-roads at the East end of the village.

Companies will be in fours outside Battn. H.Q. facing East, head of the Company resting on fork-roads ready to move as under.

    "A" Coy 6.5 p.m.
    "B" "   6.10 p.m.
    "C" "   6.15 p.m.
    "D" "   6.20 p.m.

Battn.H.Q. will march in rear of Lewis Gun sections.

3 Formation.
Battalion will move by companies at 200yds interval as far as L.35.b.5.8. As soon as the head of the leading company reaches this point the Battalion will halt. The leading platoon of the leading company, will then advance, followed by the remaining platoons of the Battalion at 200yds interval.
Lewis Gun limbers will be unloaded at L.35.b.5.8. and Lewis Gun sections will join their platoons.

4 Advance Party.
One officer and one water guide per company and a representative from each platoon will report at Battn.H.Q. at 11.0. a.m. The party will proceed to C.1 area under 2/Lieut. SPAUL who will show the officers from each company the area allotted to them. Advance party will meet the Battn. at the fork-roads at M.8.b.8.7. at Northern end of AGNY VILLAGE.

5 Halts.
ALL halts will be made East of the BAC DU NORD.

6 Completion of Move.
Completion of move will be reported to Battn.H.Q.

(Sgd) J. NICHOLS, Capt.&Adjt.
Q.V.R.

7.4.17.

7. Route. BEAUMETZ — L 35 6 5 8. — ACHICOURT — AGNY

Army Form C. 2118.

WAR DIARY

9th Bn. London Regt. Queen Victoria's Rifles

INTELLIGENCE SUMMARY.

(Erase heading not required.)

Place	Date	Hour	Summary of Events and Information	Remarks and references to Appendices
	1917 MAY 1		Battalion relieved in the line by the 2nd LONDON Regt. Digging of assembly Trenches for 2/LONDONS continued. Battalion withdrew to trenches in N.9.c.	
	2		Battalion rested during the day and moved up at midnight to assembly area West of GUEMAPPE. Road made through heavy gas shell bombardment.	
	3	3.45 a.m.	Zero hour for Third and Fifth Armies offensive. Battalion moved to assembly trenches vacated by 2/LONDONS. 2/LONDONS and L.R.13 assault CAVALRY FARM. Very heavy artillery fire on both sides. 2/Lieut. O.G. DAVIES wounded.	
		7 a.m.	"D" Coy make a bombing attack on CAVALRY FARM. Farm reported evacuated. 2/LONDONS establish in CAVALRY FARM TRENCH east of Farm and portion of LANYARD TRENCH South of ARRAS-CAMBRAI Road. L.R.13 in PIT TRENCH.	
		8 a.m.	"A" Coy in TANK TRENCH. "B", "C", & "D" Coys in GORDON SUPPORT TRENCH. Both trenches heavily bombarded. Aerial activity in all companies. Artillery continuously active on all sides.	

WAR DIARY or INTELLIGENCE SUMMARY.

Army Form C. 2118.

9th Bn. London Regt. Queen Victorias Rifles

Place	Date 1917 MAY	Hour	Summary of Events and Information	Remarks and references to Appendices
	3	5 pm	Battalion ordered to relieve 2/LONDONS in CAVALRY FARM TRENCH at 10.30 p.m. and L.R.B in LANYARD TRENCH at 1 a.m.	
		8.30 pm	Hostile Barrage put down on LANYARD TRENCH and CAVALRY TRENCH. Successful hostile counter-attack against CHERISY.	
		9.30 pm	H/LONDONS moved up to WANCOURT LINE to reinforce 169th Infantry Brigade.	
		11.30 pm	L.R.B and 2/LONDONS ordered to withdraw to CAVALRY TRENCH. Battalion relieved 2/LONDONS and L.R.B in CAVALRY TRENCH. Situation quieter. L.R.B + 2/LONDONS withdraw to trenches west of WANCOURT LINE. Q.W.R on right of this Battalion. Two Officers and 15 O.Rks of 4/ot. I.R. surrender to "B" and "D" Companies in CAVALRY FARM. A sergeant of 2/LONDONS, who had previously been its prisoner of this party, was found with them when they surrendered and released.	
	4	11 pm	Battalion relieved by the LONDON Regt. 169th of 169th Infantry Brigade less 1/Q.W.R withdraws to TILLOY Area. Battalion estimated casualties from May 1st - 110 O.Rks.	

Army Form C. 2118.

WAR DIARY

1/9th Bn London Regt. Queen Victoria Rifles.

INTELLIGENCE SUMMARY.

(Erase heading not required.)

Instructions regarding War Diaries and Intelligence Summaries are contained in F. S. Regs. Part II. and the Staff Manual respectively. Title pages will be prepared in manuscript.

Place	Date	Hour	Summary of Events and Information	Remarks and references to Appendices
	1917 MAY 5		Battalion in Trenches	
	6			
	7		in TILLOY Area.	
	8			
	9			
	10	7.30pm	Battalion relieves 1/Q.W.R. in WANCOURT LINE and came under orders of 169th Infantry Brigade as left reserve Battalion.	
	11		Battalion in reserve in WANCOURT LINE. LONDON SCOTTISH and 4/LONDONS attacked and captured TOOL TRENCH as far N as copse in N.E. Central and CAVALRY FARM TRENCH.	
	12		Battalion relieved by 1st LONDON Regt. in WANCOURT LINE and marched to Trenches in BOIS DES BOEUFS near TILLOY and came under orders of 169th Infantry Brigade.	
	13		Battalion in BOIS DES BOEUFS.	
	14		Battalion relieved 7/MIDDLESEX in WANCOURT LINE and became right	

Army Form C. 2118.

WAR DIARY or INTELLIGENCE SUMMARY.

1/9th Bn London Regt. Queen Victoria Rifles.

(Erase heading not required.)

Place	Date	Hour	Summary of Events and Information	Remarks and references to Appendices
	1917 MAY 14		reserve Battalion under orders of G.O.C. 167th Infantry Brigade.	
	15			
	16		Battalion in WANCOURT LINE. Burial parties proceed at night to clear forward area.	
	17			
	18			
	19			
	20	4:30am	Battalion relieved by 11th Royal Warwickshire Regt. and marched to huts in DUISANS.	
DUISANS	21		Inspection of clothing, arms, equipment and feet.	
	22		Inspection of H.Q. Coy by Commanding Officer. Company Training.	
	23		Company Training.	
	24	10am	Battalion marches to AGNEZ-LES-DUISANS.	
AGNEZ-LES DUISANS	25		Battalion training in all branches.	
	26			
	27			
	28		Battalion inspected by G.O.C. 56th Division and ribands presented.	

Army Form C. 2118.

WAR DIARY
or
INTELLIGENCE SUMMARY.

1/9th Bn. London Regt. Queen Victorias Rifles.

(Erase heading not required.)

Instructions regarding War Diaries and Intelligence Summaries are contained in F. S. Regs., Part II. and the Staff Manual respectively. Title pages will be prepared in manuscript.

Place	Date	Hour	Summary of Events and Information	Remarks and references to Appendices
AGNEZ-LES-DUISANS	1917 MAY 29 30 31		Battalion training in all branches.	

F. S. Follett Lieut-Colonel.
O.C. 1st Bn. Queen Victorias Rifles.

1/9th Bn London Regt. Queen Victoria's Rifles

WAR DIARY
INTELLIGENCE SUMMARY

References
Map.
51.B.S.W
1/20,000
51.B.
1/40,000
LENS 11.

Place	Date	Hour	Summary of Events and Information	Remarks
	JUNE 1917			
	1		Training at AGNEZ-LES-DUISANS.	
	2			
	3			
	4		— do —	
	5			
	6			
	7			
	8			
	9		The 169th Infantry Brigade moved to TELEGRAPH HILL AREA. The 1st Bn. Q.V.R. relieved the 8th Bn. K.R.R.C. in N.7.d.	
	10		The Battalion moved into support trenches in the right sub-sector in relief of the 2/4th ROYAL BERKS. The Battalion provided wiring parties for the 1st Bn Q.W.R.	
	11			
	12		Battalion in support.	
	13			
	14			

1/9th Bn London Regt.   Queen Victoria's Rifles   Army Form C. 2118.

WAR DIARY
or
INTELLIGENCE SUMMARY.
(Erase heading not required.)

Place	Date	Hour	Summary of Events and Information	Remarks and references to Appendices
	1917 JUNE 15		The Battalion relieved the 1st Bn. Q.W.R. in the right sub-sector.	
	16		The two advanced posts at O.26.b.05.80., O.26.b.2.9. were occupied during the night 16/17th.	
	17		During the night 17/18th the whole front covered by the 4 posts at O.20.b.3.7., O.20.b.4.3., O.20.d.4.9., O.20.d.2.7., was wired by the 5th Bn. CHESHIRE REGT. Enemy tried to rush the post at O.26.b.2.9. but were driven off with L.G. and rifle fire.	
	18		During the night 18th/19th the four posts were dug by the 5th Bn CHESHIRE REGT. and garrisoned by the Battalion.	
	19		Work was continued on the posts.	
	20		On the night of 20th/21st the Battalion was relieved in the line by the 12th Bn. the LONDON REGIMENT - The RANGERS - and marched to camp, west of BEAURAINS.	
BEAURAINS	21 22		Training in BEAURAINS.	

1/9th Bn. London Regt. WAR DIARY Queen Victoria's Rifles.

Army Form C. 2118.

or

INTELLIGENCE SUMMARY.

(Erase heading not required.)

Place	Date	Hour	Summary of Events and Information	Remarks and references to Appendices
BEAURAINS.	1917 JUNE 23			
	24			
	25		Training in BEAURAINS.	
	26			
	27			
	28			
	29			
	30			

F. B. Talbot Lieut. Colonel.
O.C. 1st Bn. Queen Victoria's Rifles.

Army Form C. 2118.

WAR DIARY
1/9th Bn. London Regt — Queen Victoria's Rifles.
INTELLIGENCE SUMMARY

Vol 32

Place	Date	Hour	Summary of Events and Information	Remarks and references to Appendices
BEAURAINS	1917 JULY 1		Battalion in Camp.	Map reference: 1/40000 Sheet 51B. M.10.b.
	2		Battalion marched from BEAURAINS to Billets in GOUY-EN-ARTOIS.	1/100000 LENS H. (B) (A)
GOUY	3		Battalion marched from GOUY-EN-ARTOIS to Billets in SUS-ST-LEGER.	(F) (4)
SUS-ST-LEGER	4 to 23		Battalion in Billets. Company training. Training of Lewis Gunners, Bombers and Rifle Grenadiers, firing on Range, Route marching, Recreational training including Battalion and Brigade Sports.	
	24		Battalion marched from SUS-ST-LEGER (leaving 7.30 am) to BOUQUEMAISON Station & entrained for WIZERNES (arriving 4.0 pm). Battalion detrained and marched to billets in NORTLEULINGHEM (arriving 11.0 pm). Battalion left VII Corps, 3rd Army and came under command of V Corps, 5th Army.	1/100000 HAZEBROUCK 5.M. (C) (4)
NORTLEULINGHEM	25 to 31		Battalion in Billets. Company training in outpost work. Battalion training in open warfare (attack, advanced guards and outposts), route marching and firing on range.	(B) (3)

L. B. Follett Lieut-Col.
Comndg. Queen Victoria's Rifles.

Vol 33

169/56

Confidential

War Diary

of

1/9th Battn The London Regt
(Queen Victoria's Rifles)

from 1st August 1917   to 31st August 1917.

9th London Regt

Army Form C. 2118.

9th Bn. London Regt. WAR DIARY or Queen Victoria's Rifles
INTELLIGENCE SUMMARY.
(Erase heading not required.)

Place	Date	Hour	Summary of Events and Information	Remarks and references to Appendices
NORTLEULINGHEM	1914 AUG. 1 to 5		Battalion training. Attack practices and outpost schemes.	
WATOU	6		Battalion entrained at WATTEN and proceeded to the WIPPENHOEK area, detraining at ABEELE. Battalion transferred to 2nd. Army Corps.	
	7		} Company training in neighbourhood of billets	
	8			
	9			
	10			
	11		Battalion moved by rail from ABEELE to OUDERDOM and marched thence to château SEGARD.	
	12		Battalion relieved the 8th Bn. Norfolk Regt. in the front line N. of the YPRES-MENIN Road, with the 1st Bn. Queen's Westminster Rifles (16th London) on the left, and this Bn. Suffolk Regt. on the right. 2nd. Lt. A.G.H.LONG was mortally wounded on the banks of the YSER Canal.	
	13		9.0 a.m. 2nd. Lt. M.C.T.BATE was killed. At 8.30 p.m. an endeavour was made to establish a line of posts in GLENCORSE WOOD. Capt. E.D.SYMES was killed and	

WAR DIARY
or
INTELLIGENCE SUMMARY.
(Erase heading not required.)

Army Form C. 2118.

Place	Date	Hour	Summary of Events and Information	Remarks and references to Appendices
	1917 AUG			
	13		2nd Lt. P.R. CALEY mortally wounded.	
	14		The Battalion was relieved by 12th Bn. London Rifle Brigade (5th hand) in the front line and withdrew to HALF-WAY HOUSE. Relief was completed by about 4.0 a.m.	
	15		Orders were received for general offensive operations on the 16th inst. 2nd. Lt. A.L. ARNOLD was killed at 6.0 p.m. At 8.0 p.m. the Bn. moved forward to an assembly area round SURBITON VILLAS. "B" Coy. were ordered to "mop up" for the L.R.B.; "A" and "C" Coys. to support the L.R.B., and "D" Coy. to hold an original front line.	
	16		At 5.45 a.m. the Fifth Army offensive operations were resumed. In spite of heavy progress at the outset under cover of a terrific creeping barrage, the 169th Inf. Bde. was compelled to withdraw to the original front line. The casualties in the Bn. were severe. The Bn. took over the right of the line at dusk, with the 1st. Bn. Q.W.R. on the left. The L.R.B. and 2nd. London Regt. were withdrawn.	
	17		The Battalion was relieved by the 4th Bn. K.R.R.C. and 5th Oxford & Bucks L.I. Relief was complete by 11.0 p.m. the Bn. withdrew to Chateau SEGARD and at 11.0 a.m. proceeded by motor buses to WIPPENHOEK area.	

Army Form C. 2118.

WAR DIARY
or
INTELLIGENCE SUMMARY.
(Erase heading not required.)

Instructions regarding War Diaries and Intelligence Summaries are contained in F. S. Regs., Part II. and the Staff Manual respectively. Title pages will be prepared in manuscript.

Place	Date	Hour	Summary of Events and Information	Remarks and references to Appendices
WATOU	1917 AUG 18 to 23		Battalion refitted, re-organised. Company training in neighbourhood of billets.	
	24		Battalion proceed by rail from ABEELE to WATTEN and marched thence to billets in SERQUES.	
	25, 26, 27, 28, 29, 30		Company training.	
	31		56th Divn. transferred to 3rd Army. Battalion marched from SERQUES, leaving at 3.30 a.m. to WIZERNES and entrained at 7.45 a.m. for MIRAUMONT arriving at 4.45 p.m. Battalion marched thence to Camp near BAPAUNE arriving at 10.0 p.m.	

Nichols, Capt. & Adjt.
for O.O. Queen Victorias Rifles
1/9th Bn London Regt.

B.M.429.

Headquarters,
56th Division.

Herewith answers received from 1/9th London Regiment, reference your G3/846.

F. Carter Pro Cyr
Brigadier General.
Commanding 169th Infantry Brigade.

20th August 1917.

Replies to G 3/846

(1) J.14.a.0.H.   2 officers 100 O.R.
(2) To dig in on Eastern edge of Glencorse Wood.
(3) Yes.
(4) No.
(7) Very good.
(11) Going was very heavy owing to ground being one mass of shell holes full of water.
(12) Enemy M.G's & snipers were very active on the right flank.
(21) 50 (approx.).
(27) Yes
(28) Attributed chiefly to (a)(c)(d)
(29) No.
(30) (a) about 6 p.m.
    (b) Enemy tried to surround & threw bombs detached post, sniped from shell holes in front & on flanks
    (c) Bombardment. Rifle fire
    (d) Yes
    (e) We retired & established strong point in the same trench nearer own front line.
(31) Enemy was able to bring enfilade fire from the right flank with his M.G's & his snipers were very active & caused casualties.

The above answers by
2/Lt J.E.N. POOLEY
"A" Co Q.V.R.

No 5 Platoon

(1) Ref. HOOGE 14.A.3040 Strength Officers 8, others [?]
(2) Mopping up.
(3) No.
(4) No.
(5) Right up to barrage
(6) Yes.
(7) Fast.
(8) Too fast
(9) Yes
(10) Held up by M.G. fire in Blockhouses
(11) Heavy going owing to shell ridden ground making advance slow
(12) Yes strong points M.G. concrete emplacements
(13) HOOGE 14.B.8045
(14) Before
(15) Yes.
(16) Yes.
   (B) Strong point Bombing & bayoneting
(17) Yes.

(17) 5 Platoons
(18) No.
(19)
(20)
  (a) Counter attack right & flank
  (b) shortage of bombs
  (c) Yes
  (d) ” ” ”
  (e)
(21) Ten winter
(22) Six ”
(23) Yes effectively
(24) Yes
(25) enemy filling from shell holes
(26) Lewis Guns acting as machine guns
(27) No quite fresh
(28)
(29) prisoners captured (15) fifteen
(30) Yes counter attacked
  (a) 6.15 am of the 16 inst
  (b) Shells machine gun fire in a [illegible] ordts enemy advanced

5. Platoon
(30) continued
 (D) Yes medium
 (E) Yes
(31) Enemy retired & prepared for counter attack leaving M.G. in strong points. Enemy strongpoints caused our advancing troops considerable trouble
(32) Enemy casualties not heavy

―――――

 Isaac Harold Lipski
 5th Platoon

Attack Report.

No. 6 Platoon. Sheet No 1

1. Map Ref. HOOGE 14a. 3070 Strength 24
2. Mopping Up
3. No.
4. No.
5. Correct distance
6. Yes.
7. Good.
8. Too fast.
9. Yes.
10. Caused by m.g. obstructions also
11. b. slow advancing over shell-riven
12. ground.
13. HOOGE 14b 9020
14. Before.
15. Unable to complete the extermination of enemy MGs in blockhouses. ~~before~~ ~~starting line tired~~
16. b. By a bombing attack from rear
17. No.

P.T.O.

Sheet No 2.

18/ No.
19/ Unable to complete mopping up ~~...~~
    ~~————————————~~
20/ Enemy counter attack on left, &
    order from 2nd London Officer.
21/ Approx 10.
22/ 5.
23/ Yes.
24/ Yes.
25/ Enemy on run, & clearing shell holes
26/ No Lewis Guns with Moppers up.
27/ No.
29/ Sent dozens of enemy to our lines
30/ Enemy counated in extended order
    & covered his attack with M.G.
    fire. We had to retire to avoid
    being cut off as our right fell
    back too.
31. Concrete blockhouses intact & guns
    still firing. ~~The~~ enemy quickly
    mounted new machine guns
    in the concrete blockhouses we
    had cleared as soon as

Sheet No 3.

our troops had evacuated the ground Had we mounted our m.g's in these concrete forts after we had taken them, we could have stopped the enemy counter attack.

32. Not as many as might be expected. Too eager to be sent over as prisoners & not enough resistance by enemy excepting his m. gunners.

A.W. Madger
Sgt.

No 7 Platoon

1. Ref HOOGE 14a. 2040 Strength 24.
2. Mopping up
3. No
4. No
5. Right up to Barrage
6. yes
7. Good
8. Too fast
9. yes
10. Held up by M G in concrete Blockhouse
11. Ground so shell torn as to making advance slow
12. Ground rough near strong point
13. HOOGE 14b. 8045
14. Before
15. yes
16. cleared by Bombing
17. yes
18. No
19. Flank attacks caused retirement by M G fire from Right
20. A
    B Shortage of Bombs
    C withdrawal of Troops off flanks. Yes
21. 12
22. 3
23. yes
24. yes
25. Retiring enemy
26. Moppers up No L.G.S
27. No
29. 10 approx
30. M G Barrage & waves in extended order from half right
31. Defences very strong as regards Redoubts
32. Medium in Number

A Frost L/c

8. Platoon B. Coy Q.V.R.

(1) Map Ref. HOOGE 14a. 2070   Strength 25.
(2) Mopping Up
(3) No
(4) No
(5) About 20 yds
(6) Yes
(7) Excellent
(8) Little to East
(9) Yes a little
(10) Owing to casualties in Platoon
(11) Heavy Going
(12) N? except for M.G. fire & Aeroplane fire
(13) HOOGE 14 b. 9020.
(14) After
(15) Yes
(16) Physically
(17) No
(18) No
(19) By being flanked on both right & left by M.G. fire

(20) Enemy attacked on Left & Right & ordered by 2' London Officer
(21) 10
(22) 4
(23) Yes
(24) Yes
(25) Enemy on Run – clearing Shell Holes
(26) No Lewis Guns with Moffer Up
(27) No
(29) Send plenty of Enemy back to our lines
(30) Enemy countered in Extended order with Overhead M.G. Barrage
(30) Had to Retire to avoid being Cut off, as our Right Flank did also
(31) Concrete Forts untouched by Shell Fire
(32) No too eager to be taken prisoner

Lce/Cpl S. Seymour.
Lce/Cpl. E. Hutchings.

9th London Regt. (Q.V.R.)

Report by "mopping up" Bn. to the Right Brigade.

1.)   Assembly carried out without difficulty.

8.)   Barrage found to be too fast.

9.)
10.)   Company fell right behind barrage, being held up by concrete blockhouses and bad going.

11.)
to)   Old Battery position J.14.b. 86 and J.14.b.90.20.
13.)

15.   Yes, caught up barrage again.

16.)
17.)   Bomb and Bayonet succeeded in taking Strong Point.

18.   No.

19.   Owing to attacks and M.G.fire from both flanks; also because unable to complete mopping up.

20. (a) Counter attacks right and left flanks.
    (b) Shortage of bombs.
    (c) Yes by order of 2nd London Officer on left flank.
    (d) M.G.fire.
    (e)
    (f)

21.   "A" Coy.   approx.   50 men.
        "B" "   "   45 men.

22.   "B" Coy.   18 men.

23.   Yes effectively.

24.   Yes.

25.   Enemy retiring and clearing shell holes.

26.   Lewis Guns where with moppers up.

27.   "A" Coy. Yes.   "B" Coy. No.

28.   "A" Coy. attributed chiefly to

    (a) Distance of the objective.
    (c) Nature of the going.
    (d) Previous exhaustion.

29.   Dozens of prisoners sent back

30.   Yes. (a) 6.15 and
                 6. 0 p.m.
        (b) Under M.G.barrage in extended order & Bombing.
        (c) M.G.Barrage.
        (d) Yes.
        (e) Yes, had to retire to avoid being cut off as troops on right had fallen back.

31. Our shell fire had no effect on his concrete emplacements. The enemy quickly mounted new machine guns in the strong points we had cleared, as soon as our troops had evacuated the ground. Had we mounted our M.Gs. in the concrete forts after we had taken them, we could have stopped the enemy counter-attacks.

32. Not as many as might have been expected. Enemy too eager to be sent back as prisoners. They scarcely made any resistance except enemy M.Gunners.

9th London Regt. (Q.V.R.)

Report by "mopping up" Bn. to the Right Brigade.

1.) Assembly carried out without difficulty.
8.) Barrage found to be too fast.
9.) Company fell right behind barrage, being held up by
10.) concrete blockhouses and bad going.
11.)
to) Old Battery position J.14.b. 86 and J.14.b.90.20.
13.)
15. Yes, caught up barrage again.
16.) Bomb and Bayonet succeeded in taking Strong Point.
17.)
18. No.
19. Owing to attacks and M.G.fire from both flanks; also because unable to complete mopping up.
20. (a) Counter attacks right and left flanks.
    (b) Shortage of bombs.
    (c) Yes by order of 2nd London Officer on left flank.
    (d) M.G.fire.
    (e)
    (f)
21. "A" Coy.   approx. 50 men.
    "B" "   "   45 men.
22. "B" Coy.   18 men.
23. Yes effectively.
24. Yes.
25. Enemy retiring and clearing shell holes.
26. Lewis Guns where with moppers up.
27. "A" Coy. Yes.   "B" Coy. No.
28. "A" Coy. attributed chiefly to

    (a) Distance of the objective.
    (c) Nature of the going.
    (d) Previous exhaustion.

29. Dozens of prisoners sent back
30. Yes. (a) 6.15 a.m and
             6. 0 p.m.
         (b) Under M.G.barrage in extended order & Bombing.
         (c) M.G.Barrage.
         (d) Yes.
         (e) Yes, had to retire to avoid being cut off as troops on right had fallen back.

31. Our shell fire had no effect on his concrete emplacements. The enemy quickly mounted new machine guns in the strong points we had cleared, as soon as our troops had evacuated the ground. Had we mounted our M.Gs. in the concrete forts after we had taken them, we could have stopped the enemy counter-attacks.

32. Not as many as might have been expected. Enemy too eager to be sent back as prisoners. They scarcely made any resistance except enemy M.Gunners.

9th London Regt. (Q.V.R.)

Report by "mopping up" Bn. to the Right Brigade.

1.)
) Assembly carried out without difficulty.
8.)

9.) Company fell right behind barrage, being held up by
10.) concrete blockhouses and bad going.

11.)
to) Old Battery position J.14.b. 86 and J.14.b.90.20.
13.)

15. Yes, caught up barrage again.

16.) Bomb and Bayonet succeeded in taking Strong Point.
17.)

18. No.

19. Owing to attacks and M.G.fire from both flanks; also
     because unable to complete mopping up.

20. (a) Counter attacks right and left flanks.
    (b) Shortage of bombs.
    (c) Yes by order of 2nd London Officer on left flank.
    (d) M.G.fire.
    (e)
    (f)

21. "A" Coy.   approx. 50 men.
    "B" "   "   45 men.

22. "B" Coy.   18 men.

23. Yes effectively.

24. Yes.

25. Enemy retiring and clearing shell holes.

26. Lewis Guns where with moppers up.

27. "A" Coy. Yes. "B" Coy. No.

28. "A" Coy. attributed chiefly to

    (a) Distance of the objective.
    (c) Nature of the going.
    (d) Previous exhaustion.

29. Dozens of prisoners sent back

30. Yes. (a) 5.15 and
           6. 0 p.m.
    (b) Under M.G.barrage in extended order & Bombing.
    (c) M.G.Barrage.
    (d) Yes.
    (e) Yes, had to retire to avoid being cut off as
        troops on right had fallen back.

31. Our shell fire had no effect on his concrete emplacements. The enemy quickly mounted new machine guns in the strong points we had cleared, as soon as our troops had evacuated the ground. Had we mounted our M.Gs. in the concrete forts after we had taken them, we could have stopped the enemy counter-attacks.

32. Not as many as might have been expected. Enemy too eager to be sent back as prisoners. They scarcely made any resistance except enemy M.Gunners.

9th London Regt. (Q.V.R.)

Report by "mopping up" Bn. to the Right Brigade.

1.) Assembly carried out without difficulty.

8.) Barrage found to be too fast.

9.) Company fell right behind barrage, being held up by
10.) concrete blockhouses and bad going.

11.)
to) Old Battery position J.14.b. 86 and J.14.b.90.20.
13.)

15. Yes, caught up barrage again.

16.) Bomb and Bayonet succeeded in taking Strong Point.
17.)

18. No.

19. Owing to attacks and M.G.fire from both flanks; also
because unable to complete mopping up.

20. (a) Counter attacks right and left flanks.
(b) Shortage of bombs.
(c) Yes by order of 2nd London Officer on left flank.
(d) M.G.fire.
(e)
(f)

21. "A" Coy.   approx. 50 men.
    "B" "   "   45 men.

22. "B" Coy.   18 men.

23. Yes effectively.

24. Yes.

25. Enemy retiring and clearing shell holes.

26. Lewis Guns where with moppers up.

27. "A" Coy. Yes.   "B" Coy. No.

28. "A" Coy. attributed chiefly to

    (a) Distance of the objective.
    (c) Nature of the going.
    (d) Previous exhaustion.

29. Dozens of prisoners sent back

30. Yes. (a) 5.15 and
          6. 0 p.m.
    (b) Under M.G.barrage in extended order & Bombing.
    (c) M.G.Barrage.
    (d) Yes.
    (e) Yes, had to retire to avoid being cut off as
        troops on right had fallen back.

31. Our shell fire had no effect on his concrete emplacements. The enemy quickly mounted new machine guns in the strong points we had cleared, as soon as our troops had evacuated the ground. Had we mounted our M.Gs. in the concrete forts after we had taken them, we could have stopped the enemy counter-attacks.

32. Not as many as might have been expected. Enemy too eager to be sent back as prisoners. They scarcely made any resistance except enemy M.Gunners.

9th London Regt. (Q.V.R.)

Report by "mopping up" Bn. to the ~~Right~~ Centre Brigade.

1.) Assembly carried out without difficulty.
8.) Barrage found to be too fast.
9.) Company fell right behind barrage, being held up by
10.) concrete blockhouses and bad going.
11.)
to) Old Battery position J.14.b. 86 and J.14.b.90.20.
13.)
15. Yes, caught up barrage again.
16.) Bomb and Bayonet succeeded in taking Strong Point.
17.)
18. No.
19. Owing to attacks and M.G.fire from both flanks; also because unable to complete mopping up.
20. (a) Counter attacks right and left flanks.
    (b) Shortage of bombs.
    (c) Yes by order of 2nd London Officer on left flank.
    (d) M.G.fire.
    (e)
    (f)
21. "A" Coy.   approx.   50 men.
    "B" "   "   45 men.
22. "B" Coy.   18 men.
23. Yes effectively.
24. Yes.
25. Enemy retiring and clearing shell holes.
26. Lewis Guns where with moppers up.
27. "A" Coy. Yes. "B" Coy. No.
28. "A" Coy. attributed chiefly to

    (a) Distance of the objective.
    (c) Nature of the going.
    (d) Previous exhaustion.

29. Dozens of prisoners sent back
30. Yes. (a) 6.15 am.
             6. 0 p.m.
         (b) Under M.G.barrage in extended order & Bombing.
         (c) M.G.Barrage.
         (d) Yes.
         (e) Yes, had to retire to avoid being cut off as troops on right had fallen back.

/31.

31. Our shell fire had no effect on his concrete emplacements. The enemy quickly mounted new machine guns in the strong points we had cleared, as soon as our troops had evacuated the ground. Had we mounted our M.Gs. in the concrete forts after we had taken them, we could have stopped the enemy counter-attacks.

32. Not as many as might have been expected. Enemy too eager to be sent back as prisoners. They scarcely made any resistance except enemy M.Gunners.

56

1/9 London Regt
Vol XVI

Vol 34

<u>Confidential</u>

169/56

<u>War Diary</u>

of

<u>1/9th Bn The London Regt</u>

from 1st September 1917   to 30th September 1917

Army Form C. 2118.

WAR DIARY
or
INTELLIGENCE SUMMARY.

1/9th Bn London Regt. Queen Victoria's Rifles

(Erase heading not required.)

Instructions regarding War Diaries and Intelligence Summaries are contained in F. S. Regs., Part II. and the Staff Manual respectively. Title pages will be prepared in manuscript.

Place	Date	Hour	Summary of Events and Information	Remarks and references to Appendices
	1916 SEPT.			
BAPAUME	1		Battalion in camp at H.35 c.8.3. ref. 1/40,000 Sheet 57c	
	2		Company and Specialist training	
	3			
	4		Inspection by IV Corps Commander.	
	5		Battalion moved into Brigade Reserve at LEBUCQUIÈRE ref. 1/40,000 Sheet 57c. I.Z.4 and 30.	
LEBUCQUIÈRE	6			
	7		1 Company in support to 1st London Rifle Brigade, 1 Company in support to 1st Queen's Westminster Rifles.	
	8		Remainder of Bn., Company and Specialist training. Firing on Range.	
	9			
	10			
	11			
	12		Battalion relieved 1st Queen's Westminster Rifles in trenches, LOUVERVAL SECTOR (Right Sub-Sector) 3 Companies in Front Line + Posts, 1 Company in Support. 1 Company 1st Q.W.R. also in Support.	
	13			

WAR DIARY
or
INTELLIGENCE SUMMARY.
(Erase heading not required.)

Army Form C. 2118.

Place	Date	Hour	Summary of Events and Information	Remarks and references to Appendices
	1914 SEPT.			
	14 to 20		Battalion in Trenches.	
	20		Battalion relieved by 1st Queens Westminster Rifles & moved into Divisional Reserve at I.29.a.	
	21			
	22 to 28		Company & Specialist training. Firing on Range. Attack Practice.	
	29		Battalion relieved 1st Queens Westminster Rifles in LOUVERAL Right Sub-Sector.	
	30		Battalion in trenches. 3 Companies in front Line & Posts, 1 Company in Support. 1 Company 1st London Rifle Brigade also in Support.	

Wilson
Capt. & Adjt.
for O.C. Queen Victorias Rifles
1/9th Bn. London Regt.

Confidential

Vol 35

War Diary

of

1/9th Bn. The London Regt.

from 1st October 1917   to 31st October 1917.

Army Form C. 2118.

WAR DIARY

1/9th Bn. London Rifles or Queen Victoria's Rifles

INTELLIGENCE SUMMARY.

(Erase heading not required.)

Instructions regarding War Diaries and Intelligence Summaries are contained in F. S. Regs., Part II. and the Staff Manual respectively. Title pages will be prepared in manuscript.

Place	Date	Hour	Summary of Events and Information	Remarks and references to Appendices
	1914 OCT.			
	1 to 6		Battalion in trenches – LOUVERVAL Right Sub-Sector.	
	7		Battalion relieved by 1st Queen's Westminster Rifles and moved into Brigade Reserve.	
	8 to 14		1 Company in support to 1st London Rifle Brigade. 1 Company in support to 1st Queen's Westminster Rifles. Remainder of Bn. in Hutments. Company & Specialist training. Firing on Range.	
	15		Battalion relieved 1st Queen's Westminster Rifles in trenches, LOUVERVAL Right Sub-Sector.	
	16 to 21		Battalion in trenches.	
	22		Party of 1 Officer + 50 Other Ranks attempted a raid on enemy post at K.8.a.central. (ref 9/40000 Sheet 57 C) Enemy found on the alert and raiding party were driven off after inflicting casualties on the enemy. Casualties to raiding party- 1 Officer + O.Rks. wounded, all brought back to our lines.	
	23		Battalion relieved by 1st Bn. Queen's Westminster Rifles and moved into Divisional Reserve at I.29.d.	

Army Form C. 2118.

WAR DIARY
or
INTELLIGENCE SUMMARY.
(Erase heading not required.)

Instructions regarding War Diaries and Intelligence Summaries are contained in F. S. Regs., Part II. and the Staff Manual respectively. Title pages will be prepared in manuscript.

Place	Date	Hour	Summary of Events and Information	Remarks and references to Appendices
	1914 OCT. 2.14 to 31		Company and Specialist Training. Firing on Range. Bombing, Lewis Gun and Musketry Tests.	

Wiseman
Capt. & adjt.

For O.C. Queen Victoria's Rifles.
1/9th Bn. London Regt.

CONFIDENTIAL

YM36

WAR DIARY

1/9th LONDON Regt.

NOVEMBER 1917

35807. W16879/M1879 500,000 3/17 R.T. (1074) Forms/W3091/3   Army Form W.3091.

Cover for Documents.

Nature of Enclosures.

Notes, or Letters written.

Army Form C. 2118.

WAR DIARY

1/9th Bn. London Regt. Queen Victoria's Rifles

INTELLIGENCE SUMMARY.

(Erase heading not required.)

Instructions regarding War Diaries and Intelligence Summaries are contained in F. S. Regs., Part II. and the Staff Manual respectively. Title pages will be prepared in manuscript.

Place	Date	Hour	Summary of Events and Information	Remarks and references to Appendices
LEBUCQUIERE	1914 NOV 1		Battalion relieved 1/Queens Westminster Rifles in LOUVERVAL Right Sub-Sector.	By. 1/40000 Sheet 57c I.30.
	2 to 7		Battalion in trenches.	
	8		Battalion relieved by 1/Q.W.R. northdrew to Brigade Reserve, H.Q. & 2 Companies to hutments in LEBUCQUIERE, 1 Company in support to 1/Q.W.R, 1 Company in support to 1/L.R.B.	
	9 to 15		Battalion in Brigade Reserve. Working parties engaged on repairing roads &c.	
	16		Battalion relieved 1/Q.W.R in LOUVERVAL Right Sub-Sector.	
	17 to 18		Battalion in trenches.	
	19		Battn. H.Q. moved to TROUT (K.Y.C.0.5)	
	20	6.20am	Bn. went down to smoke barrage. Attack on CAMBRAI commenced. Evening - Patrols sent out & established contact with division on Right. Posts established on CAMBRAI Road. Bn. H.Q. moved to STURGEON (J.6.6.9.3)	
	21		1 Company knocked up enemy outpost line & captured 1/prisoners and 1 light machine gun.	
	22		Posts held on CAMBRAI Road.	

Army Form C. 2118.

WAR DIARY
or
INTELLIGENCE SUMMARY.
(Erase heading not required.)

Instructions regarding War Diaries and Intelligence Summaries are contained in F. S. Regs. Part II. and the Staff Manual respectively. Title pages will be prepared in manuscript.

Place	Date	Hour	Summary of Events and Information	Remarks and references to Appendices
	1914 Nov 23		Division on Right advanced & Bn. Posts were withdrawn. Bn. engaged on digging Communication trench from J.5.V.4.5 to D.30.V.0.Y.	
	24/25		Battalion relieves 2nd London Regt. (R.F.) in front line.	
	26		Front line consolidated.	
	27		3.0 p.m. Bn. "Stood to" on S.O.S. being sent up by Bn. on left, who reported enemy attack which followed.	
	28		Situation quiet.	
	29		Battalion was relieved by 2nd London Regt. & withdrew to original front line.	
	30		Battalion "Stood to" at 10.30 a.m. 2 Companies moved up to support 2nd London Regt. and 2 Companies to support 1/QWR.	

Truly
Capt & Adjt.
for O.C. Queen Victorias Rifles.
9th Bn. London Regt.

35807. W16879/M1879 500,000 3/17 R.T. (1074) Forms W3091/3 169/56   Army Form W.3091.

Cover for Documents.

Nature of Enclosures.

CONFIDENTIAL

WAR DIARY

1/9th LONDON REGT (Q.V.R)

DECEMBER, 1917.

Notes, or Letters written.

Army Form C. 2118.

1/9th Bn. London Regt. **WAR DIARY** Queen Victoria's Rifles.
or
INTELLIGENCE SUMMARY.

(Erase heading not required.)

Instructions regarding War Diaries and Intelligence Summaries are contained in F. S. Regs., Part II. and the Staff Manual respectively. Title pages will be prepared in manuscript.

Place	Date	Hour	Summary of Events and Information	Remarks and references to Appendices
	1914 DEC.			
	1		Battalion withdrawn from HINDENBURG LINE to LOUVERAL. Ref. 1/40000 Sheet 57d J.10.a.q.8.	
	2		Battalion withdrawn to O'SHEA Camp. Ref. 1/40000 Sheet 57d. I.7.q.d.	
	3		Battalion marched from O'SHEA Camp to FREMICOURT where they entrained at 10.30 a.m. for BEAUMETZ, marching thence to BERNEVILLE. Ref. 1/40000 Sheet 51d. Q.6.d.	
	4		Battalion in Camp at BERNEVILLE	
	5		Battalion marched from BERNEVILLE to Camp at ST CATHERINE. Ref. 1/40000 Sheet 51 B.3.a.central.	
	6		Battalion in Camp at ST CATHERINE	
	7		169th Bde. relieved 92nd Bde. in the Line. Battn. moved into Support relieving 12th Bn. E. Yorks. Regt. Bn. H.Q. & 2 companies in ROUNDHAY Camp, 2 companies in RED LINE.	
	8		Battalion relieved 11th Bn. E. Yorks Regt. in Left (R2) Sub-Sector.	
	9 to 13		Battalion in trenches. Improvement of trenches and wiring carried out.	
	14		Battalion relieved by 1st Bn. London Rifle Bde. moved into Brigade Support, Bn. H.Q. & 2 companies in ROUNDHAY Camp, 2 companies in RED LINE.	
	15 to 19		Battalion in Brigade Support. R.E. Working parties & work on support trenches. Work on wire "concertinas" in Camp.	

WAR DIARY
or
INTELLIGENCE SUMMARY.
(Erase heading not required.)

Army Form C. 2118.

Place	Date	Hour	Summary of Events and Information	Remarks and references to Appendices
	1914 DEC. 20		Battalion relieved 1st Bn. London Rifle Brigade in Left Sub-Sector	
	21 to 23		Battalion in trenches. Improvement of trenches and wiring carried out.	
	24		Battalion relieved by 1st Bn. London Rifle Brigade and moved into Divisional Reserve at AUBREY Camp, ROCLINCOURT. Ref. 1/40000 Sheet 51B G.4.a.1.6.	
	25 to 27		Battalion in camp.	
	28		Battalion relieved 1st Bn. London Rifle Brigade in Left Sub-Sector.	
	29 to 31		Battalion in trenches	

Nichols
Capt. & Adjt.
for O.C. Queen Victoria's Rifles.

Confidential.

War Diary
of
1/9th Bn. London Regt., Queen Victoria's Rifles

From 1st January 1918
to 30th January 1918

Volume I

Army Form C. 2118.

WAR DIARY
or
INTELLIGENCE SUMMARY.
(Erase heading not required.)

Place	Date	Hour	Summary of Events and Information	Remarks and references to Appendices
	1918 Jan 1		Battalion relieved in GAVRELLE left sub-sector by 1st Bn. London Rifle Brigade and withdrew to RED LINE reserve trenches.	
	2 to 9		Battalion in RED LINE. Works made C.E. XIII Corps.	
	10		Battalion withdrew from RED LINE and entrained at ECURIE Railhead for AUBIGNY.	
	11 to 29		Marching thence to billets in CAMBLIGNEUL. Company and Battalion training. Musketry on range. Field firing.	
	30		Battalion disbanded. 5 Officers, 130 Other Ranks transferred to 13th London Regt. 12 Officers 250 Other Ranks transferred to 16th London Regt. 4 Officers 46 Other Ranks transferred to 4th London Regt. Commanding Officer & Transport Officer awaiting orders of 58th Divn. Remainder of Bn. amalgamated with 2/9th Bn. London Regt.	

Nicholl
Capt & Adjt.

for O.C. 1/9th Bn. London Regt.
"Queen Victoria's Rifles."

www.ingramcontent.com/pod-product-compliance
Lightning Source LLC
Chambersburg PA
CBHW081430160426
43193CB00013B/2241